Flavors of a Newport Summer

A collection of local recipes and artwork

that celebrates the best of summer life in *Newport*

St. Michael's Country Day School
Parent Association

ST. MICHAEL'S
COUNTRY DAY
SCHOOL
1938   NEWPORT

*T*aste and enjoy the essence of a *Newport* summer

Brian Becken, "An Afternoon at the Beach"

Brian Becken's formal art training began at the age of fourteen when he attended summer school classes at the Corcoran Museum School, in Washington, D.C. While earning a degree in English Literature at Reed College, he took several studio art classes. After college he became interested in the paintings of the American Impressionists. He returned to school to study drawing and painting at Rhode Island School of Design, the Art Student's League, and at the atelier of Robert Cormier in Boston.

Although Brian paints a variety of subject matter, the recurrent theme is figures in outdoor settings. He is most known for his paintings of New England beaches, including several in Newport. Having lived in Newport, Brian has included many local families in his beach scene paintings. His paintings are in many collections throughout North America. Brian lives in Providence and his paintings can be found in Newport at Roger King Fine Arts.

A Newport Summer Moment...

"I love feeling the sun on my back in late summer after a soaking rain. In my garden, all varieties of tomatoes — lady girl reds, yellows pears, pink heirlooms, beefsteaks — are bursting with moisture and sweet as honey.
At the same time, the pepper plants — green wonders, yellow Hungarian waxes, classic jalapenos, ripening red and orange Italian sweets — are dripping with color, flavor, and spicy heat. I pick them all with reverence along with pungent garlic bulbs, sweet onion, fragrant cilantro and create salsa that Liz, our four kids, and I devour with appreciation."

— Emlen Drayton

Acknowledgements

There are so many people to thank for their contribution to the publication of this book. In large ways and small, from the early concept stages to the final days before printing, members of our Cookbook Committee, the Parent Association Board, Administration, and others have been committed to this project and have played pivotal roles in bringing this book to reality. On behalf of myself and St. Michael's Country Day School, I want to thank them for their support, their countless hours of volunteer work and their dedication to this project and our school.
Bethany Di Napoli, Chair, Cookbook Committee

Cookbook Committee Members

Lydia Babich, Sarah Bartlett, Greer Beecroft, Monique Burgess, Jacqueline Colbert, Jill Cooper, Anne Corbin, Debbie Crocker, Heather de Pinho, Kim Doherty, Nancy Estrada, Colleen Everett, Tamara Farrick, Shelly Ferrall, Daniela Frater, Sharon Gallipeau, Julie Janson, Carla Lawrence, Kimberly Lugo, Sandra MacDonald, Marianne Menas, Victoria O'Loughlin, Judith Owens, Krista Peterson, Sheila Powell, Peggy Richmond, Merritt Robinson, Barbara Roos, Lori Russell, Johna Toppa

Parent Association Board

Sarah Bartlett, Monique Burgess, Diane Canepari, Chris Di Napoli, Jill Gudoian, Andy Kagan, Sheila Powell

Head of School
Whitney Slade

Special Thanks

To Leslie Fisk, for embracing this project and coordinating the outstanding student artwork; we are all grateful to you.
To Pieter Roos and Christine Wirges, for your time and expertise in photographing the artwork.
To Misi Narciso and Emily Potts who provided technical assistance and graphic design expertise;
you know this book would not have happened without your help.
To Katelyn O'Grady and Tom Ring of Meridian Printing whose patience and assistance in this project have been truly valued.
To Claire Coombs, Tara Gnolfo, Mardi Sayer, Leslie Thurston, and Betsy Walker for your marketing and administrative assistance.
To our sponsors, Bank Newport, Franklin & Co., Greenvale Vineyards, Mansions & Manors, Newport Harbor Corp., and Wimco; we would not have been able to publish this book without your support.
To the students of St. Michael's Country Day School, you created the inspiring art pieces which are the pride and joy of this book.
And lastly, to the parents, faculty and staff who took the time to submit recipes and personal reflections for this cookbook, your contributions have given this book a unique personal touch that we can all be proud of.

Summer in Newport is...

"-beach towels stacked by the door
-sand on the floor of my car
-yellow light bulbs in my porch fixture
-the slam of a screen door
-picnics at the beach, for breakfast, lunch or dinner
-the thrill of riding a wave all the way in to shore
-the sound of jazz from Fort Adams or Mozart from a mansion
-the thwack of a tennis ball and the smack of a golf ball
-buying sweet native corn from the guy in the truck
-a cool swim before breakfast and after work
-the smell of tar and diesel down on the docks
-watching a thunderstorm go by
-taking a nap on the porch couch
-Mason jars full of sea glass and shells
-jumping off the stern of a boat while rafting with friends
-sails in the harbor
-the squeal of children running through a sprinkler
-picking a ripe tomato from my garden
-watching a baseball game at Cardine's Field
-a refreshing shower after a day spent by the water
-hamburgers and hot dogs on the grill
-scarlet red geraniums and Nikko blue hydrangeas
-buying precooked lobsters at Aquidneck Lobster Co.
-falling asleep to the sound of crickets
-the night air perfumed with honeysuckle

While you can find all of these things elsewhere, it's only in *Newport*
that you can find them all!"

— Mardi Sayer

Contents

Foreward   6

Breakfast at Gooseberry Beach   7

Flower Show Garden Brunch   17

Lunch on Center Court   29

Jazz Festival Picnic   41

4th of July Cookout   53

Tailgate at the Polo Match   67

Sunset Sail Cocktails and Hors D'oeuvres   79

Orchestrating a Bellevue Dinner   89

Cliff Walk To-Go   105

Traditional Newport Clambake for 20   110

St. Michael's Country Day School   114
Contributing Restaurants and Inns   116
Artists and Galleries   118
Downtown Newport Map   120
Recipe Index   122

Foreward

This book began with the simple idea of collecting recipes from the families of St. Michael's Country Day School—a nursery through Grade 8 independent school in Newport, Rhode Island—and incorporating them into a cookbook whose proceeds would benefit our school. Thanks to the creative talents of our cookbook committee members, that idea evolved into the book you hold in your hands: *Flavors of a Newport Summer*.

Capturing the essence of a glorious Newport summer, the book features favorite recipes from our families, faculty, and staff, as well as from the best restaurants in Newport, arranged in themed chapters devoted to the activities and events that we think make our City by the Sea so special. For artwork, we looked no farther than our school's own students, whose delightful illustrations enliven the pages within every chapter. We also invited local artists to contribute artwork, and those illustrations introduce each chapter. And we added personal reflections from those of us who are inspired every day by the unique qualities of our city.

The end result is a book meant to be a recipe-rich celebration of what we love about Newport in the summer. From Flower Show Garden Brunch to Jazz Festival Picnic, each chapter is filled with little treasures to help you savor the vitality of a summer in Newport – whether you are here or far away. A Newport summer is never out of reach as long as *Flavors of a Newport Summer* is close at hand.

We thank you for supporting our students and the educational mission of our school through your purchase of this book. Our committee is proud to share this book with you. May the flavors, sights, and smells of a Newport summer grace your days all year long!

Warmest regards,

Bethany DiNapoli
Chair, Cookbook Committee
St. Michael's Country Day School

Breakfast at Gooseberry Beach

Kate Hoyt Pzoki

No trip to Newport is complete without a visit to Gooseberry Beach. Located on scenic Ocean Drive, Gooseberry, named for Gooseberry Island just off shore, is sheltered from the ocean currents and receives gentle waves—an ideal setup for children and grownups alike. At this local favorite, you can catch crabs in the tidal pool, take time to build an amazing sandcastle, or stroll the sun-speckled sand while beachcombing for shells. After working up an appetite you can visit the gourmet snackbar for a delicious lunch or special treat. A perfect day at the beach!

About the Artist

Kate Hoyt Psaki, "Red Umbrella"

Kate is an alumnae of St. Michael's Country Day School and was the valedictorian of her class in 1954. Kate has been painting all her life; her parents and siblings are well known artists themselves. She studied art both at Rhode Island School of Design and the Art Center in Los Angeles. Kate has won numerous awards for her work, including awards from the Greenwich Art Club, Darien Art Association and Spring Bull Gallery in Newport. She is living and working as an artist here in Newport and remembers St. Michael's as the best years of her youth. "Red Umbrella" is an oil on panel. It is a little 'pleine aire' jewel. Gooseberry Beach is a favorite place for Kate to paint because of the wonderful islands.

Kate's paintings can be found in Newport at Arnold Art Gallery and Newport Fine Arts.

8

Breakfast at Gooseberry Beach

MENU SELECTIONS

Auntie Pam's Banana Bread
Streusel Coffee Cake
Best-Ever Blueberry Muffins
Fruit and Nut Breakfast Bars

Creamy Strawberry French Toast
Gaufrettes
Torta Rustica
Cajun Breakfast Casserole
Spinach & Cheese Mini Quiche

Summer Fruit Salad with Mint Sugar

Auntie Pam's Banana Bread

2 ripe bananas, mashed
1 1/2 cup sugar
1/3 cup vegetable oil
1 tsp baking soda
1 tsp vanilla
2 eggs
1 3/4 cup flour
1 cup chopped walnuts (optional)
3/4 cup plus 1 tbsp buttermilk
1/8 tsp salt

Preheat oven to 325°.

1. Grease and flour 8 x 4 inch bread loaf pan. Combine all ingredients and mix well.

2. Fill pan about half way or a little more. Bake for 60-80 minutes until top is golden brown.

   Yield: 1 loaf

Allison deHorsey

"This is the moistest banana bread ever. Very easy to make, too!"

Streusel Coffee Cake

Coffee Cake:
1/2 cup salted butter
1 cup sugar
2 eggs
1 cup sour cream
2 cups flour
1 tsp baking powder
1 tsp baking soda
1 tsp vanilla

Topping:
1/4 cup sugar
1 tsp cinnamon
1/2 cup pecans or walnuts, coarsely chopped

Preheat oven to 350°.

1. Cream butter, sugar, eggs, sour cream together in a mixer.

2. Add vanilla and mix well.

3. Add dry ingredients.

4. Mix topping ingredients together.

5. Pour half of batter into greased spring form bundt pan and sprinkle with half the topping. Pour remainder of batter into pan and add remaining topping. Bake for 40-45 minutes.

   Serves: 8-10

Beverly Little

Best-Ever Blueberry Muffins

Muffins:
1/2 cup sugar
1/4 cup butter, softened
1 egg
2 1/2 cup flour
4 tsp baking powder
1/2 tsp salt
1 cup milk
1 tsp vanilla
1 1/2 cup blueberries

Crumb topping:
1/2 cup sugar
1/2 tsp cinnamon
2/3 cup flour
1/4 cup butter, cold

Preheat oven to 375°.

1. In a mixing bowl, cream sugar and butter until fluffy. Add egg and mix.
2. In separate bowl, combine flour baking powder and salt. Add dry ingredients to sugar/egg mixture, alternating with the milk.
3. Add vanilla and mix. Gently fold in blueberries, spoon mixture into greased muffin tins.
4. For topping, mix together in a small bowl until crumbly, the sugar, cinnamon, flour and butter. Sprinkle over muffins.
Bake for 20-25 minutes.

Yield: 12 muffins

Susan Kehoe

"Fresh blueberries are a true summer treat. These muffins are so good, and will surely become a family favorite."

Fruit & Nut Breakfast Bars

3 cups quick oats
2 cups coconut, shredded
1 cup almonds, sliced
1/2 cup walnuts, chopped
1 cup raisins & cranraisins, combined
1/4 cup wheat germ
1/4 cup sesame seeds
1/2 cup dried apricots, chopped
1/2 cup pitted dates, chopped
1/2 cup flour
1/2 tsp salt
3/4 cup honey
1/2 cup vegetable oil
3 eggs, slightly beaten

Preheat oven to 350°.

1. Combine oats, coconut, almonds and walnuts, wheat germ, and sesame seeds in large roasting pan. Bake 18 minutes, stirring once. Cool well.
2. Combine oat mixture with raisins, cranraisins, dates, apricots, flour and salt in large bowl.
3. Stir in eggs, honey and oil, mixing well.
4. Press mixture into two well-greased, 8-inch square baking pans. Bake for 20 minutes or until set.
5. Cut into 2-inch squares while warm. Cool in pans on rack. Store in tightly wrapped foil.

Yield: 32 bars

Claire Stieff

"These delicious squares are a family favorite. They are healthy and full of flavor."

Breakfast at Gooseberry Beach

2ND GRADE, CLASS OF 2012

Creamy Strawberry French Toast

1 loaf of French bread, sliced
10 eggs
8 oz cream cheese
1 1/2 cup half & half
1/4 cup maple syrup
8 tbsp butter, melted
2 cups fresh strawberries, sliced
2 cups strawberries, frozen
1/4 cup sugar

1. Layer bread in 9 x 12 inch pan. Cut cream cheese into small pieces and layer over bread. Cover with remaining bread.
2. Mix eggs, half & half, syrup and butter. Pour mixture over bread and cover. Refrigerate overnight.
3. Place strawberries and sugar in bowl. Mix well. Cover and refrigerate overnight.
4. Bake for 40 minutes at 350°. Garnish with strawberry mixture.

Serves: 6

Darlene Ward

Gaufrettes

Belgian Waffles

4 1/2 cups all purpose flour
1/2 cup sugar
1 tsp cinnamon or 1 tsp vanilla extract
2 tsp baking powder
3/4 lb sweet butter, softened
4 eggs
2 tbsp rum (optional)

1. Sift dry ingredients into a bowl. Make a well in the center and put the butter, eggs and rum into the well. Gradually mix the dry ingredients into the wet ingredients; it will be a paste consistency.
2. Let the mixture stand at room temperature, uncovered for 2 hours. Divide into small balls and cook on a hot, waffle iron coated with cooking spray.
3. Cool on a rack.
Topping suggestions: confectioners sugar, sliced strawberries with whipped cream, marmalades or jam.

Serves: 4-6

Ellyn Eaves-Hileman
"Gaufrettes were one of my family's favorite treats when we lived in Belgium. We miss them!"

13

Torta Rustica

2 1/4 cups all purpose flour
3/4 cup yellow cornmeal
1/2 tsp salt
3/4 cup cold butter or margarine cut into
   small pieces
3 large eggs, divided
3-4 tbsp cold water
12 oz skim milk ricotta cheese
4 oz feta cheese
1 cup parmesan cheese, grated
2 tbsp finely chopped fresh basil
2 cups shredded mozzarella cheese
8 oz thinly sliced prosciutto ham
1 jar (7 oz) roasted red peppers
1 can (15 oz) artichoke hearts
1/2 lb asparagus, trimmed, lightly steamed

Preheat oven to 375°.

1. Crust: Mix flour, cornmeal, salt in large bowl. Cut in butter with pastry blender until mixture forms coarse crumbs. In a separate small bowl, beat eggs with 3 tablespoons water. Stir into mixture until dough holds together (add water if dry). Shape 2/3 dough into flattened round, repeat with remaining dough. Wrap and refrigerate at least 30 minutes until firm. Roll out 2/3 dough portion on floured surface to 15-inch diameter - place in ungreased 8- or 9-inch springform pan, pressing sides and bottom lightly. Trim overhang to within 1-inch rim. Dough scraps can be rolled again and cut in decorative shapes for top crust.

2. Make ricotta mixture by combining ricotta, feta, Parmesan, 2 eggs and basil.

3. Assembly: Scatter half of mozzarella over bottom. Arrange half of prosciutto. Spread with half of ricotta mixture. Cover with half of roasted peppers and half of artichokes, add remaining mozzarella and prosciutto. Add remaining ricotta mixture, top with asparagus arranged in a spoke. Add remaining peppers and artichoke hearts.

4. Roll out remaining dough to 9-inch circle. Place on top of filling to cover. Moisten edge with water and seal. Crimp edges. Brush top and decorative shapes with lightly beaten egg. Cut several small slits in top crust.

5. Bake for one hour or until crust in golden brown and pulls away from sides. Cool for 45 minutes, remove from pan and cool completely. Serve at room temperature.

Serves: 12

Judy Owens

"Very colorful, nice for a buffet."

Cajun Breakfast Casserole

1 tbsp vegetable oil
1 lb andouille sausage or Chorizo, chopped
1 bunch scallions, sliced thinly
1 cup onion, diced
1/4 cup celery, diced
1/2 cup red pepper, diced
1/2 cup green pepper, diced
1 tbsp garlic
6 whole eggs
2 cups heavy cream
2 cups milk
1 tbsp kosher salt
2 tsp Paul Prudhommes Cajun Seasoning
8 cups cubed French bread
2 cups grated cheddar cheese

Preheat oven to 375°.

1. Heat vegetable oil in a large skillet. Saute scallions, onion, celery, peppers, garlic and sausage for 3 -5 minutes or until onions are translucent.
2. Whisk eggs, milk and cream with salt and Cajun seasoning. Set aside.
3. Mix the bread cubes with the sausage mixture and half of the cheese. Spread evenly in a 3-qt buttered casserole.
4. Pour egg mixture over the bread cubes, sausage and cheese. Spread remaining cheese on top.
5. Bake 40 -45 minutes. Let rest 10 minutes before serving and indulging!

Serves: 8-10

What a way to wake up after a night of summer fun in Newport. The Cheeky Monkey Café's casserole will definitely fire you up!

A *Newport* Summer Moment...

"On a summer morning when you're walking down to the beach, breathing the fresh clean air, and feeling the warmth of the sun penetrating your bare skin, and seeing the ocean sparkle from the reflection of the sun... it's enough to take your breath away. It reminds you of the long winter you just endured when the frigid cold air took your breath away and you thought seriously about moving south. But at this moment, right now, its all worth it and there's nowhere else you'd rather be."

-Trish Lang

Spinach - Cheese Mini Quiche

1/2 stick butter
3 eggs
1 cup milk
1 tsp salt
1 tsp baking powder
1 lb Monterey Jack cheese, shredded
1 package chopped frozen spinach

Preheat oven to 325°.
1. Melt butter in 13 x 9 inch pan.
2. Thaw spinach at room temperature or defrost in microwave. Squeeze out excess water and set aside.
3. In bowl, beat eggs. Add milk, flour, salt, and baking powder. Mix well. Add cheese and spinach. Bake for 30-35 minutes or until light golden brown on top.
4. Let set and cool. Cut into squares or triangles. These can be frozen and reheated at 325° for 12-15 minutes.

Serves: 6-8

Gail Ruggieri

*"I find these freeze well. Adults and children love these.
My grandchildren actually love them, too!"*

Summer Fruit Salad with Mint Sugar

1/4 cup loosely packed fresh mint
3 tbsp sugar
1 1/4 lb blackberries
3 firm-ripe medium peaches or
  nectarines, pit removed, cut into
  wedges
1/2 lb seedless green grapes
  (1 1/2 cups), halved

1. Pulse mint and sugar in a food processor until finely ground. Sprinkle mint sugar over fruit in large bowl and toss gently to combine. Let stand 5 minutes before serving.

Serves: 6

Michele Scott

Flower Show Garden Brunch

Newport Flower Show

Each June, the Newport Flower Show at Rosecliff Mansion, boasts a premier outdoor flower show event. Enjoy judged floral designs and horticultural offerings, lectures, demonstrations, daylong children's programs and amusements galore. Dining is available on the oceanside lawn of Rosecliff, along with a shopper's paradise, the Garden Marketplace. The event supports the work of the Preservation Society of Newport County. Wear your most festive, floral hat and breathe in the heady scent of summer!

About the Artist

Eveline Roberge, "Newport Flower Show"

Eveline Roberge's work evokes a mood of nostalgia that seems to be the product of fanciful imagination. In truth, careful research, consideration of form and composition of all structures and villages, and an eye for architectural precision combine with a very personal view of the people, animals and a natural setting.

Although Eveline currently lives in Newport, her heritage is Bristol, England. Ironically, her first mural panorama was a three-fold screen of Bristol, Rhode Island, which still remains with the John Winthrop De Wolf family. Eveline's murals grace many locations in Newport including the Sheffield Huntington House, Old Nat's House, and the Sanford-Covell House in the historic section of Newport known as "The Point." Her paintings and prints are in numerous private collections in England and America. Eveline's paintings and prints can be found in Newport at Fisher Gallery.

Flower Show Garden Brunch

MENU SELECTIONS

Fresh Mushroom Soup

❧

Brie and Cherry Pastry Cups
Crab Stuffed Bacon Wrapped Shrimp

❧

Baby Spinach Salad with Warm Goat Cheese Medallions
Salad of Potatoes, Avocado and Watercress

❧

Grandma Barb's Tahoe Brunch Pudding
Artichoke Oven Omelet
Spinach Stuffed Sole with Lemon Zest Sauce

❧

Dutch-Style Belgian Endive
Sweet Minty Carrots
Vegetarian Quinoa Casserole
Spinach Soufflé

❧

Coconut Cream Pie
Summer Peach Crisp
Lemon Meringue Pie

Fresh Mushroom Soup

7 tbsp butter
1 lb fresh mushroom, sliced for varying
  thickness
3 tbsp flour
2 cups chicken broth
1/2 cup beef broth
3/4 cup milk
juice of one lemon
1/2 cup heavy cream (optional)
3 tbsp fresh parsley, chopped
salt & pepper to taste

1. Melt 2 tablespoons butter and sauté mushrooms for about 5 minutes over medium heat and set aside.
2. In a large, heavy saucepan slowly melt remaining butter; add the sifted flour and mix with whisk.
3. Gradually add broths, milk, lemon and cream, if used.
4. Add mushrooms, salt and pepper to taste. Just before serving, add parsley.

Serves: 4

Jane Hence

"My children, their friends, and now my grandchildren, have this often by special request; it is elegant enough and delicious enough for a fancier occasion."

A Newport Summer Moment...

"I love going in the ocean at the beach. The water feels salty and the waves splash me. I love to build drippy sand castles."

-Anna Ming Holden PK-4

Brie and Cherry Pastry Cups

36 pre-formed frozen pastry puffs,
  thawed
1/3 to 1/2 cup red cherry preserves
4 oz Brie cheese, cut into 36,
  1/2 inch square pieces
1/4 cup chopped pecans
2 tbsp chopped fresh chives

Heat oven to 375°.

1. Bake pastry puffs for 10 minutes. Press center with handle of wooden spoon. Bake 6-8 minutes longer or until golden brown. Immediately press again in center.
2. Fill each with about 1/2 teaspoon preserves. Top with cheese piece, pecans and chives.
3. Bake 3-5 minutes or until cheese in melted. Serve warm.

Yield: 36 pieces

Wendy Lambert

"These are delicious and always a hit."

Crab Stuffed Bacon Wrapped Shrimp

with Key lime glaze and rum soaked mangoes

Shrimp
20 unpeeled Shrimp
2 bacon strips per shrimp

Crabmeat Mixture
1 lb lump crabmeat
2 tbsp ground ginger
1 tbsp ground white pepper
1 egg
1/4 cup coarse ground Japanese bread-crumbs (known as Panko)
1/4 cup sour cream
3 tbsp lemon juice
4 scallions, sliced diagonally (white and green parts)
2 roasted red peppers, diced

Rum Soaked Mangoes
2 mangoes, diced
1 red pepper, diced
1 jalepeno pepper, seeds removed, diced
1 shallot, minced
1 tbsp black sesame seeds
4 tbsp honey
4 tbsp coconut rum

Key Lime Glaze
1/2 cup key lime juice
3 tbsp light corn syrup

Preheat oven to 350°.

1. Prepare crabmeat mixture. Combine the egg, sour cream, lemon juice, scallions, red peppers and seasonings together in a large bowl. Gently fold in the crabmeat. Be careful not to break up the lumps. Gently mix in the breadcrumbs. The mixture will be slightly wet. Set aside.

2. Prepare the shrimp. Peel and butterfly the shrimp and then stuff with a tablespoon of the crabmeat mixture. Carefully wrap two bacon strips around each shrimp, overlapping the two strips so that the crabmeat does not fall out. Set aside.

3. Prepare mangoes. Combine all ingredients in a bowl and set aside.

4. Combine ingredients for the Key lime glaze in a separate bowl and set aside.

5. Final presentation:
Add 1 tablespoon olive oil to a sauté pan, on medium high heat. Add stuffed shrimp and sear until golden brown on the outside. Place on a baking pan and cook at 350 degrees until bacon is crisp, about 15 - 20 minutes. Once removed from the oven, pour or brush the Key lime glaze onto the shrimp.

6. To serve, place 2 tablespoons of rum soaked mango on a serving plate. Arrange shrimp on the plate and enjoy! Serve with a very light Sauvignon Blanc.

Serves: 4

This recipe from Asterisk is a good marriage of Caribbean ingredients. It is great for summer parties, cocktail parties, and to wow your good friends.

Baby Spinach Salad with Goat Cheese

Goat Cheese Cakes
1/4 cup water
1 egg mixed with water
6 two-oz medallions goat cheese
1 cup panko bread crumbs, toasted
1/2 cup ground toasted almonds
1/2 bunch chives, finely cut

Vinaigrette
3/4 cup olive oil
1/3 cup aged sherry vinegar
1/4 cup orange juice concentrate
2 shallots, finely diced
3 tbsp fresh tarragon
pinch salt & pepper

Salad
3 oranges, peeled and cut into segments
1/2 cup sliced blanched almonds, toasted
9 cups baby spinach leaves

Preheat oven to 350°.

1. For goat cheese cakes, prepare six, 2-ounce medallions of goat cheese.
2. Combine egg and water and dip goat cheese medallions into egg wash.
3. Combine almonds, chives and panko bread crumbs. Roll medallions in this mixture and bake for 8 minutes to warm.
4. For vinaigrette, blend together all ingredients and add salt and pepper to taste.
5. For salad assembly, toss 9 cups cleaned baby spinach in dressing and top with oranges and almonds. Put warm goat cheese medallions on top.
      Serves: 6

Pamela Chapman
"Excellent as a first course or with soup on the patio for lunch."

Salad of Potatoes, Avocado and Watercress

1 1/2 lb small new potatoes
1 large ripe avocado
3 bunches cress, washed
2-3 tbsp olive oil
1-2 lemons, juiced
salt and freshly ground pepper

1. Cook the new potatoes in salted water until tender, drain. Slice any larger sized potatoes in half, leaving smaller ones whole.
2. Slice the avocado in half, remove pit. Slice it lengthwise into thick slices or chunks and place in a bowl. Add potatoes to the avocado.
3. Add the cress, olive oil and lemon juice. Season and toss. Serve on a big plate or platter. Scatter additional cress on top.
      Serves: 4-6

Shelly Ferrall

Grandma Barb's Tahoe Brunch Pudding

12 slices whole-wheat bread
3 tbsp butter, softened
1/2 cup butter
1 lb fresh mushrooms, trimmed & sliced
2 cups yellow onion, thinly sliced
1 1/2 lbs mild Italian sausage
3/4 cup grated cheddar cheese
5 eggs
2 1/2 cups milk
1 tsp dry mustard
3 tsp Dijon mustard
1 tsp ground nutmeg
1 tsp salt
1/2 tsp pepper
2 tbsp Italian flat-leaf parsley, finely
   chopped

1. Butter the bread with the softened butter and set aside.
2. In a large skillet, melt the butter. Sauté the mushrooms and onions over medium heat until tender. Season to taste with salt and pepper and set aside.
3. Cook the sausage and cut it into bite-sized pieces.
4. In a greased 11 x 17 inch shallow casserole, layer half the bread, half the mushroom mixture, half the sausage and half the grated cheese. Repeat the layering, ending with the cheese.
5. In a mixing bowl, whisk together the eggs, milk, mustards, nutmeg, salt and pepper. Pour over the layered ingredients. Cover and refrigerate overnight.
6. Sprinkle parsley evenly over casserole and bake at 350°, uncovered for 1 hour.

Serves: 8

Barbara Roos

*"Good and easy to make. I used white bread, but I'm sure
you could use whole wheat, French, etc. "*

Samuel Durfee House

Artichoke Oven Omelet

1 14-oz can artichoke hearts, drained,
   chopped
2 cups grated taco blend or 'Mexican'
   cheese
1/4 cup Parmesan cheese, grated
6 eggs
1 cup sour cream

Preheat oven 350°.
1. Spray or butter 9-inch deep dish pie plate. Fill with chopped artichokes and Mexican cheese, lightly toss together. Sprinkle Parmesan cheese over top.
2. In a bowl beat the eggs and sour cream until combined. Pour mixture over artichokes and cheese. Bake, uncovered, for 25-30 minutes until knife in center comes out clean. Let stand for 5 minutes before serving.

Serves: 4 - 6

Samuel Durfee House

Flower Garden

PRE-K 4, CLASS OF 2015

Spinach Stuffed Sole with Lemon Zest Sauce

1 1/2 lbs sole
1 bag of fresh baby spinach, washed, chopped
2 garlic cloves, peeled and smashed
1 tbsp olive oil
2 tbsp dry sherry
1 tbsp grated Parmesan cheese
salt and pepper to taste
2 tsp parsley, chopped

Lemon Zest Sauce:
1/2 cup light mayonnaise
1/3 cup fresh grated Parmesan
1 1/4 tsp Worcestershire
1/4 cup lemon zest from 1 large lemon
1 tbsp lemon juice
salt and pepper to taste

Preheat oven to 400°.

1. Sauté chopped spinach and garlic in olive oil until spinach is barely wilted, but not browned. Add cheese and sherry, salt and pepper to taste and set aside.

2. Prepare sauce by combining all ingredients.

3. Spread small amount of spinach mixture on each fillet, roll fillet and place in a greased pyrex dish, seam side down. Spoon sauce over each rolled fillet.

4. Bake for 15 minutes. Sprinkle parsley over fish and broil 4-5 minutes or until sauce browns.

Serves: 3-4

Kathleen Kits van Heyningen

Dutch-Style Belgian Endive

6-10 small Belgian endives
12-20 very thin slices of Westphalian ham or good quality prosciutto
1/2 cup shredded mozzarella
1/2 cup shredded (white) cheddar cheese
1/2 cup grated gouda cheese
Italian bread crumbs

Preheat oven 350°.

1. Rinse endive thoroughly, cut off bottom. Place in a pan of cold water, cover completely with water and boil for 5-10 minutes until soft when forked. Place in colander to drain. Depending on size of endive, cut the lengthwise in half or quarters (spears).

2. Spray pyrex dish with cooking spray. Wrap each endive spear with ham and place in pyrex dish. Cover with cheeses equally. Lightly sprinkle bread crumbs over cheese.

3. Bake for 10-15 minutes until cheese melts and starts to bubble. Serve hot.

Serves: 6

Kathleen Kits van Heyningen

Sweet Minty Carrots

1 large bag baby carrots
1 tbsp butter
1 tbsp honey
1/4 cup fresh mint leaves, chopped
salt and pepper to taste

1. Place carrots in large sauce pan just submerged in water. Boil gently until tender, drain.
2. Add the butter and honey. Stir and simmer on low for flavors to blend, about 5 minutes.
3. Add mint, salt and pepper. Toss and serve.
Serves: 6-8

Sandy MacDonald

Vegetarian Quinoa Casserole

1 bell pepper, diced
1 sweet Vidalia onion, diced
2 stalks celery, diced
2 carrots, diced
2 zucchini or summer squash, diced
1 eggplant, diced
6 cloves garlic, minced
olive oil for sauteeing, about 1/3 cup
4 tbsp butter
2-3 tbsp flour
1 quart vegetable broth
24 oz grated cheeses including:
    cheddar, Jack, Parmesan, Romano,
    Manchengo or sheep/goat milk
paprika, to taste
1 tbsp curry paste
2 cups broccoli florets
2 cups cauliflower florets
1/2 lb assorted wild mushrooms
1 oz porcini mushrooms, dried, soaked
    and cleaned (optional)
2 cups quinoa, soaked, parboiled
    10 minutes, drained

Preheat oven to 300°.

1. Sauté pepper, onion, celery and carrots in 3 Tbsp oil; set aside.
2. Sauté zucchini, eggplant and garlic in 3 Tbsp oil; set aside.
3. Prepare roux in casserole pan: Melt butter; when bubbling, whisk in flour. Very important: whisk constantly 5-10 minutes over low/medium heat being careful not to burn flour.
4. Prepare volute sauce: After flour starts to brown in color, slowly whisk in vegetable broth. As sauce thickens, add cheeses and whisk briskly over low heat until mixture is smooth. If cheese becomes stringy, just keep stirring making sure cheese doesn't stick and burn on pan bottom. Season volute with paprika, curry paste, salt and pepper to taste.
5. Add remaining ingredients and stir mixture completely. If necessary, add more vegetable stock. Cover and bake 1 hour. Garnish with fresh herbs of your choice and serve hot.
Serves: 8-10

Robert Kalaidjian

"Curry paste is optional, but try Patak's Biryani or Hot Curry in a bottle, it's really good. Recipe serves 8 as a main course, 10 as a side dish."

Spinach Soufflé

1 10-oz package frozen creamed spinach, thawed
3/4 cup coarsely grated Swiss cheese
1/4 tsp salt
1/4 tsp pepper
2 large egg yolks
3 large egg whites

Preheat oven to 400°.

1. Butter 9-inch diameter glass pie dish. Blend creamed spinach, grated Swiss cheese, salt and pepper in medium bowl; whisk in egg yolks.
2. Using electric mixer, beat egg whites in large bowl until stiff but not dry; fold into spinach mixture. Gently transfer to prepared dish.
3. Bake soufflé until beginning to color at edges and center is puffed and softly set, about 18 minutes.

Serves: 4-6

Kathleen Glassie

"Sounds heavy but is actually light and airy.
Great served with crispy artesian bread."

Coconut Cream Pie

Pie:
2 chocolate cookie pie crusts
2 cups milk
1 cup heavy cream
2 large whole eggs
2 large whole yolks
3/4 cup sugar
4 oz, shredded coconut
1 tsp vanilla

Topping:
2 cups heavy cream
1/2 cup confectioners sugar
1/4 cup toasted coconut

Preheat oven to 350°.

1. Pie filling: Scald milk and heavy cream, let cool.
2. Beat eggs and sugar in a mixer. Add the cooled milk and cream in a stream to the egg mixture. Beat with a mixer on low speed. Stir in coconut and vanilla. Pour in pie shells.
3. Bake for 35-40 minutes or until set. Cool completely before adding topping.
4. Topping: Beat cream and confectioners sugar until peaks form. Spread over pies. Top with toasted coconut. Keep refrigerated until ready to serve.

Serves: 16, makes 2 pies

Karen Andrade

" May prepare crust using 1 1/2 cups chocolate wafer crumbs mixed with 6 tablespoons
butter, melted. Press evenly into pie pan. Bake 10 minutes at 350°."

Summer Peach Crisp

1/2 cup butter, softened
6 cups ripe peaches, sliced and peeled
1/2 cup packed brown sugar
1/2 cup flour
3/4 cup rolled oats
1/2 tsp cinnamon
1/2 tsp nutmeg

Preheat oven to 375°.

1. Spread 2 tablespoons butter in bottom of shallow 1 1/2 quart baking dish; arrange peaches in even layer.

2. Combine brown sugar, oats, flour, spices. Blend in remaining butter with fork until mixture is crumbly.

3. Sprinkle mixture evenly over peaches; press lightly with fork. Bake for 30-40 minutes until fruit is tender.

Serves: 6-8

Elizabeth Baxter

"Can substitute apples, but best with peaches."

Lemon Meringue Pie

1 frozen ready-to-bake deep dish pie crust

Filling:
1 1/3 cup sugar
1/3 cup cornstarch
6 large egg yolks (reserve whites)
1/2 cup fresh lemon juice (grate zest first)
3 tbsp grated lemon zest
3 tbsp cold butter cut into small pieces

Meringue:
6 egg whites
1/2 tsp cream of tartar
3/4 cup sugar

Preheat oven to 450°.

1. Pre-bake frozen pie crust as package directs for a one-crust pie. Reduce oven to 350°.

2. Filling: mix sugar with cornstarch in a 2 quart saucepan. With whisk, stir in 1 1/2 cup lukewarm water, the yolks and juice. Stirring, bring to a gentle boil and let boil for 1 minute until translucent and thick. Remove from heat. Stir in zest and butter until butter melts. Pour into crust.

4. Meringue: Beat egg whites and cream of tartar in a large bowl on low speed until soft peaks form. Increase speed to medium-high and add sugar, 1 tablespoon at a time, beating just until stiff peaks form.

5. Spoon meringue over filling to cover, mounding in center. Swirl meringue decoratively.

6. Bake 20 minutes until browned and meringue temperature registers at least 160°. Cool, then refrigerate at least 2 hours.

Serves: 8

Susan Kehoe

"This is a tart-sweet, cold, refreshing pie that is perfect on a hot, seabreeze filled day!"

Lunch On Center Court

Tennis, anyone? Even if you don't play, come visit The International Tennis Hall of Fame at the Newport Casino, site of the first U.S. National Championships in 1881. Housed in the Newport Casino, one of the finest examples of Victorian Shingle-style architecture in the world, is the International Tennis Hall of Fame Museum. The museum is the largest tennis museum in the world and presents an exciting chronology of the sport's rich history, from its origins up to today's superstars. If you are a tennis fan, come here in July to see the only ATP professional men's tennis tournament played on grass courts in North America. It's a winner!

About the Artist

Peter Hussey, "Lunch at Center Court"

Peter Hussey began painting after moving to Rhode Island in 1990. The state's architectural diversity, epitomized in the Shingle style, called to him and remains his subject of choice. As a self-taught painter, he very much wears the hat of the student, not only of watercolor technique, color, and composition, but of the means to effectively balance the representational with the abstract. Taking guidance from a thoughtful author about "never repeating the same variation twice," Peter continues to explore the work of different American artists as the means to bring dynamic strength and freshness to his paintings. A three-time winner of the Watercolor Prize at the Newport Art Museum's Annual Members Exhibition, Peter serves on the Board of the Art League of Rhode Island and is also a member of the American Artist's Professional League in New York City. His paintings can be found at The Harrison Gallery in Williamstown, Massachusetts, where he had his second one-man show in September 2005.

Lunch on Center Court

MENU SELECTIONS

Spiced Pear Bloody Mary Mix

Norey's Fabulous Corn Chowder
Chilled Fruit Soup with Fresh Mint

Lobster Martini

Sweet Summer Salad
Watermelon Tomato Salad

Grilled Marinated Shrimp with Mango Lime Relish
Sea Scallops with Pear, Endive and Maytag Blue Cheese
Sautéed Chicken Breasts with Balsamic Vinegar Sauce

Creamy Two Cheese Polenta
Café Green Beans
Wild Rice Salad

Creamy Blueberry Pie
Simple Simon's Frozen Pieman's Yogurt Pie

The Spiced Pear's Bloody Mary Mix

2 bulbs fennel, diced
2 large sweet onions, diced
1 bunch celery hearts, diced
2 cloves garlic, smashed
2 cans tomato juice
12 drops Tabasco sauce
2 tbsp Worcestershire sauce
1 tsp celery seeds
2 tbsp Dijon mustard
fresh dill
1/8 cup fresh lemon juice
1/8 cup Ouzu -Japanese lemon juice
   (optional)
black pepper and sea salt to taste

Preheat oven to 300°.

1. Combine fennel, onions, celery hearts and smashed garlic in a bowl. Transfer to a baking pan and roast slowly until translucent and soft, about 30 minutes. Let cool.
2. In a food processor or blender, puree the roasted vegetables with the remaining ingredients.
3. Serve with vodka (or serve without, as a "virgin"). Garnish with celery sticks.

"The Bloody Mary recipe is an intriguing one that sets the Spiced Pear apart from other recipes as some of the ingredients are roasted in a low oven giving the mixture a great texture and tang."

Norey's Fabulous Corn Chowder

1 lb of bacon
2 tbsp butter
1 cup onions, chopped
1 cup fresh corn
1 cup celery, chopped
1 qt of chicken broth
1 14 oz can of creamed corn
2 large potatoes, peeled and cubed
1 qt heavy cream
2 tbsp fincely chopped dill for garnish

1. Fry bacon separately, crumble and set aside.
2. Sauté the onions, fresh corn, and celery in butter until the onions are translucent and the corn has caramelized.
3. Add the chicken broth, potatoes and creamed corn. Cook until the potatoes can be easily pierced with a fork, approximately 15 minutes.
4. Slowly add the heavy cream to the mixture and continue simmering for an additional 15 minutes.
5. Serve the soup piping hot with a fabulous garnish of freshly chopped dill.

Serves: 6

Comfort foods with a gourmet twist and a home-like atmoshpere make you want to stay at Norey's all day. This corn chowder recipe is a classic!

Chilled Fruit Soup with Fresh Mint

2 cups pineapple-coconut fruit juice blend
1/2 ripe banana
1/2 green apple, peeled
juice of one lemon
1 fresh mint leaf
1 peach, peeled, chopped
1 pear, peeled, cored and chopped
1 cup plain yogurt

1. Combine all ingredients in food processor or blender.
2. Cover and refrigerate for 4 hours or preferably overnight. Soup will thicken.
3. Serve in bowls garnished with fresh berries and dusting of cinnamon or nutmeg with mint leaves.
Serves: 4

Jane Carey

Sakonnet Fish Company

Lobster Martini

1 lb of fresh or frozen lobster meat, (cooked)
1 cup of lettuce chopped
4 cups of Cole slaw spiced with a pinch of cracked black pepper
8 green olives
4 small wooden skewers
4 martini glasses

1. Place 1/4 cup of chopped lettuce in each martini glass.
2. Add 1 cup of spiced Cole slaw to each glass, then add four ounces of cooked lobster meat to each glass.
3. Finally, garnish each salad with a pair of green olives pierced with a wooden skewer.
Serves: 4

The award-winning Lobster Martini is one of the most popular items on the menu at The Sakonnet Fish Co. Presented in a martini glass with an olive garnish, the lobster salad is a great appetizer or lunch item.

Sweet Summer Salad

10 oz Romaine lettuce
1 cup strawberries, sliced
3 tbsp sugar
3 tbsp mayonnaise
2 tbsp milk
1 tbsp poppy seeds
1 tbsp white vinegar
2 oz honey roasted almonds

1. Wash and chop lettuce. Toss with sliced strawberries.
2. Mix sugar, mayonnaise, milk, poppy seeds, and vinegar together and toss with salad. Top with almonds.

Serves: 4

Heather dePinho

Watermelon Tomato Salad

4 lbs red/yellow seedless watermelon,
    cut into cubes
30 red grape tomatoes, halved
30 yellow cherry tomatoes, halved
20 small basil leaves
2/3 cup olive oil
2 tbsp sugar

1. Mix watermelon, tomatoes, and basil. Top with olive oil.
2. Add sugar and season with salt and pepper.

Serves: 12

Krista Peterson

A Newport Summer Moment...

"I love sharing our summer with friends and family that come to visit. For them, spending the day on or by the water is therapeutic. The "icing on the cake" is coming home to a lobster dinner on our deck!"

-Lori Russell

Grilled Marinated Shrimp with Mango-Lime Relish

Shrimp:
1 1/2 lbs of 16-20/lb size shrimp, shell on
  and butterflied (split)
24 oz pineapple juice
1 cup dark rum
1 cup fresh lime juice (approximately
  6 limes)
1 clove elephant garlic, chopped
4 tbsp fresh cilantro, chopped
dash of hot pepper sauce

Relish:
2 bell peppers, red and yellow
1 vidalia onion
4 kiwis
1 mango
1 splash lime juice
4 avocados

1. Mix pineapple juice, rum, lime juice, garlic, cilantro, and hot sauce in a large pyrex baking dish. Add rinsed shrimp and cover. Refrigerate up to 2 or 3 hours.

2. Skewer shrimp and place on medium high grill for 3-5 minutes per side. Drizzle marinade on shrimp while cooking.

3. Peel and halve avocados and remove pits. Scoop out insides of avocado gently, to keep in tact and create "bowl".

4. Finely chop peppers, onion, kiwis and mango, then mix in a large bowl, adding a splash of lime juice. Ladle fruit/vegetable mixture into avocado halves and serve on plate with grilled shrimp.

Serves: 4

Jay Willis

"This dish goes well with a side of Basmati rice with saffron.
For you 'year-round grillers' it's a taste of the Caribbean here in New England!"

A Newport Summer Moment...

"The Rommel family has had a cabana on third beach for decades. The first one was well-known by artists who painted it until Hurricane Bob washed it away. This year ends the 30 year summer-time memories, as the Norman Bird Sanctuary creates a beautiful and natural environment. Third Beach meant:
lobsters and clams for the family and staff cooked by my husband;
my mother-in-law Mary's special 3-bean salad;
our children learning to swim and growing too old for the baby beach;
windsurfing and driftwood fires;
taking my St.Georges' classes to paint there; the ever changing surface and landscape of the beach;
walking down to the shack at the beach club for lunch as the sand burns your feet and the sun warms your skin;
and gathering the clan year after year as the other cabana neighbors became friends."

-Sandy Rommel

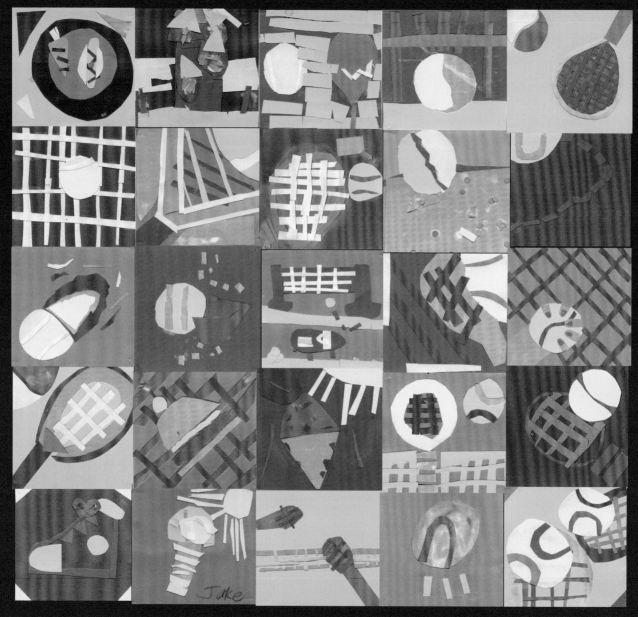

Tennis Anyone?

GRADE 4, CLASS OF 2010

Sea Scallops with Pear, Endive and Maytag Blue Cheese

1 red pepper
3 tbsp extra virgin olive oil
2/3 tsp each of herb seed blend
   (white pepper, fennel, coriander)
1 lb sea scallops
2 Belgian endives (1 white, 1 red)
2 pears (1 red, 1 green), sliced
1 head frisee lettuce, torn
2 oz Maytag blue cheese
1 tbsp aged balsamic vinegar
2 tsp olives, chopped
1 shallot, minced
salt and pepper to taste

1. Roast, peel and seed the red pepper.
To Roast Pepper: Broil pepper about 2 inches from heat, turning it every 5 minutes, for 15 to 20 minutes, or until skins are blistered and charred. Transfer peppers to a bowl and let stand, covered, until cool enough to handle. Keeping peppers whole, peel them, starting at blossom end. Cut off pepper tops and discard seeds and ribs.

2. Puree in a blender with 1 tablespoon olive oil. Set aside.

3. Place the herb blend onto a baking pan and roast at 400° for approximately 10 -15 minutes. Remove from oven and place into a bowl or use a mortar and pestle. Grind herbs into a fine consistency.

4. Coat the scallops in the herb mixture.

5. In a non-stick sauté pan at medium high heat, sauté the scallops in 1 tablespoon of olive oil. Set aside.

6. Wash and separate the endive leaves. On a serving plate, arrange the endive leaves in a fan shape at the top half of the plate, alternating the two colors. Arrange slices of pear among the endive, alternating colors again.

7. Onto the center of each plate, place equal amounts of frisee. Divide the Maytag blue cheese, minced shallot, olives, vinegar and tablespoon of olive oil into four portions and sprinkle on top of each frisee.

8. Slice scallops in half - fanning five pieces in the foreground. Add red pepper mixture near the scallops. Enjoy!

Serves: 4

Summer in Newport is not complete without a visit to The Black Pearl on the wharf. Daniel Knerr, Executive Chef, has kindly shared this fantastic recipe.

Sautéed Chicken Breasts with Balsamic Vinegar Sauce

1/2 cup chicken broth
1/2 cup balsamic vinegar
2 tsp honey
1 tbsp butter
1 tbsp vegetable oil
4 (5-oz) skinless, boneless chicken breast
   halves
1/4 tsp salt
1/4 tsp freshly ground black pepper
1/4 cup all-purpose flour
2 tbsp finely chopped shallots
Chopped parsley (optional)

1. Combine broth, vinegar, and honey and set aside.
2. Melt butter and oil in a large nonstick skillet over low heat.
3. While butter melts, sprinkle chicken with salt and pepper. Place flour in a shallow dish. Dredge chicken in flour; shake off excess flour.
4. Increase heat to medium-high; heat 2 minutes or until the butter turns golden brown. Add chicken to pan; cook 4 minutes on each side or until golden brown. Remove chicken from pan; keep warm.
5. Add shallots and sauté 30 seconds. Add the broth mixture, scraping to loosen browned bits. Bring to a boil, and cook until reduced to 1/2 cup (about 3 minutes). Serve sauce over chicken. Garnish with chopped parsley, if desired.

Serves: 4

Monique Burgess

*"Done in record-time and tastes like it took hours.
Great when paired with an orzo or polenta."*

Creamy Two-Cheese Polenta

4 cups 1% low-fat milk
1 cup water
1 1/4 tsp salt
1/4 tsp freshly ground black pepper
1 1/4 cups instant dry polenta
1/3 cup Mascarpone cheese
1/3 cup grated Parmigiano-Reggiano cheese

1. Combine milk, water, salt and pepper in a medium saucepan over medium-high heat. Bring to a boil; gradually add polenta, stirring constantly with a whisk.
2. Cook 2 minutes or until thick, stirring constantly. Remove from heat; stir in cheeses. Serve immediately.
3. If you're not serving this immediately, keep the polenta warm by covering it and placing it over very low heat. Stir occasionally. Mascarpone ensures the polenta's creamy consistency and rich flavor.

Serves: 8

Monique Burgess

*"One of my kids favorites! This pairs nicely with any main course accompanied by a
strong-flavored sauce (especially balsamic vinegar). It comes together very quickly, so
don't wander away or you may come back to find a polenta-crusted stove."*

Café Green Beans

1 lb fresh green beans
2 tbsp extra virgin olive oil
3-4 cloves garlic
2 tsp sesame seeds
juice of one lemon
1-2 tbsp soy sauce
freshly ground pepper to taste

1. Rinse and trim beans. Place them in large sauce pan with water to cover. Bring to boil, boil for 3 minutes, drain, set aside.
2. Turn stove to medium-low and add oil, garlic, and sesame seeds. Sauté until garlic is golden. Add lemon juice and soy. Toss in beans, mix well, cook one more minute. Add pepper and serve.

Serves: 6

Sandy MacDonald

"Had this dish at a bistro in Chapel Hill, NC."

Wild Rice Salad

1/2 lb wild rice (about 1 1/2 cups), rinsed
2 celery ribs, 1/4-inch diced
2 small vine-ripened tomatoes, seeded and 1/4-inch diced
1/2 carrot, 1/4-inch diced
1/2 red onion, chopped fine
1/2 red bell pepper, 1/4-inch diced
1/2 green bell pepper, 1/4-inch diced
1/2 yellow bell pepper, 1/4-inch diced
1/2 cup sliced almonds, toasted until golden
1/2 cup raisins
6 tbsp balsamic vinegar
3 tbsp vegetable oil
1 tsp minced garlic

1. In a large saucepan bring 5 cups salted water to a boil. Add wild rice and cook, uncovered, stirring occasionally, until tender, about 40 minutes.
2. Drain wild rice and transfer to a bowl to cool. Chill wild rice, covered, until cold, about 2 hours.
3. In a large bowl combine vegetables, almonds, and raisins; toss with wild rice.
4. In a bowl whisk together vinegar, oil, garlic, and salt and pepper to taste until combined well. Pour dressing over salad and toss well.

Serves: 6

Krista Peterson

"Salad may be made 2 days ahead and chilled, covered."

Creamy Blueberry Pie

Crust:
1 1/2 cup flour
1 1/2 tsp sugar
1/2 tsp salt
1/2 cup canola oil
3 1/4 tbsp milk

Filling:
4 cups fresh blueberries
2/3 cup sugar
1/4 cup flour
1/2 tsp cinnamon
pinch salt
1/3 cup milk
2/3 cup heavy cream

Whipped cream:
1 cup heavy cream
confectioners sugar,
   to taste

Preheat oven to 400°.

1. To prepare crust: In a 9-inch pie pan, combine all ingredients and stir with a fork until blended. Using your fingers, press the dough into pan and all the way up the sides, making a smooth rim with your fingers. Use a fork to prick bottom of crust to prevent bubbling.

2. To prepare filling: Rinse berries in a colander and remove any soft ones. Spread them out on a towel to dry slightly, then pour them into pastry shell. In medium bowl, combine sugar, flour, cinnamon and salt. Add milk and cream and whisk until smooth. Pour mixture over berries. Bake for 40-45 minutes or until set. After 25 minutes, cover edges with aluminum foil to prevent them from getting too dark. Let cool on wire rack, then refrigerate for at least 2 hours or until well chilled.

3. To prepare whipped cream: In a deep bowl, whip cream until soft peaks form. Gradually stir in confectioners sugar. Serve in a bowl on side so guests can help themselves.

Serves: 8

Sharon Goldstein

Simple Simon's Frozen Pieman's Yogurt Pie

1 1/4 cups of graham cracker crumbs
1/4 cup sugar
1/2 cup soft butter
1 8-oz package of cream cheese, softened
1 8-oz container of strawberry or
   lemon yogurt
1 10-oz package of frozen sliced strawberries,
   thawed
fresh sliced strawberries or peaches

Preheat oven to 400°.

1. Mix the graham cracker crumbs and sugar together in a bowl. Add the softened butter and stir well with a fork until crumbly. Press this mixture into and 8- or 9-inch pie pan. Bake for 8 minutes.

2. Blend the softened cream cheese with the yogurt in a bowl until it is smooth. Add the strawberries and their syrup to the cheese mixture.

3. When the crust in cool, pour in the filling and carefully put it in the freezer. Before you serve the pie, arrange the fresh fruit on top in a pretty design.

Serves: 6

Elaine Lindh

Jazz Festival Picnic

Newport Jazz Festival

On a mid-July weekend in 1954, the "First American Jazz Festival" debuted in Newport, RI. An assorted collection of musicians and fans gathered for the inaugural show, which featured performances by Ella Fitzgerald, Dizzy Gillespie, and Billie Holiday, among others. The Jazz Festival was born. Founded by nightclub owner and musician George Wein, the festival has spanned the entire spectrum of jazz with big band, modern, gospel, Dixieland and even fusion. The Newport Jazz Festival has evolved into a three-day jazz spectacular featuring both legendary and cutting-edge jazz musicians. Come blow your horn at the Newport Jazz Festival — it happens every August at Fort Adams State Park.

About the Artist

James Allen, "This Thing Called Jazz"

When James Allen began his series of jazz paintings in 1999, he was about 14 years old. He thought it was necessary to paint with respect to passion. For him, that passion was music. The jazz theme was inspired by his love of concert, symphonic, and jazz ensembles as well as Pablo Picasso's cubist painting, 'Los Tres Musicos.' Although James did not begin to develop a style until much later, the rhythms, syncopations, and sounds grabbed him right away. Today, he continues to paint the passion of music through an explosion of color and rhythm. In the summer of 2005, James' work was solely exhibited at Virginia Tech's Perspective Gallery, a national and international art gallery. In addition, his work was featured on the cover of an international music CD, The Best Polish Jazz 2005. James currently attends Virginia Tech in Blacksburg, Virginia, where he studies mechanical engineering. His paintings can be viewed on his website at www.jamesallenart.com.

Jazz Festival Picnic

Menu Selections

Marinated Shrimp Wrapped in Snow Peas
Ginger Scented Pecans

Jazzy Chicken Salad
Lemon and Artichoke Salad

Spicy Supercrunchy Fried Chicken
The Best Ribs Ever

Provencal Potato Salad
Nutted Wild Rice
Microbrew Beer Bread

Creole Bread Pudding
Watermelon with Mango and Lime
Macadamia Lime Pie
Gingersnaps
Turtle Bars

Lemonade by the Sea

Marinated Shrimp Wrapped in Snow Peas

1 bay leaf
1 lb medium shrimp, peeled and deveined, tail on
1 tbsp champagne vinegar
1/4 cup olive oil
1 tbsp rice wine vinegar
1 large garlic clove, crushed
20 tender, young snow peas

1. Bring a large pot of salted water and bay leaf to a boil. Add shrimp and cook for about 2 minutes; until pink and cooked through. Drain shrimp and put in glass bowl to set aside.
2. Combine vinegars with oil and garlic. Pour mixture over shrimp; stir to coat well. Cover dish with plastic wrap and refrigerate for 1-2 days.
3. String the snow peas and blanch in boiling water for 30 seconds.
4. Split the pods lengthwise and wrap a pea pod half around each shrimp and fasten with a toothpick. Serve cold or at room temperature.

Serves: 6-8

Elizabeth Gallagher
"Can do ahead! Not only easy, but beautiful and delicious!"

Ginger Scented Pecans

5 cups pecan halves
1/2 cup sugar
2 tsp kosher salt
1 tsp ground ginger
2 tbsp honey
2 tsp canola oil

Preheat oven to 325°.

1. Place nuts in a single layer on one large baking sheet. Toast until fragrant, about 12 minutes, rotating pan and stirring pecans halfway through.
2. Combine sugar, salt, ginger in a small bowl; set aside.
3. Combine honey, oil and 2 tablespoons water in a 2-3 quart saucepan. When pecans are toasted, bring honey mixture to a boil. Add the pecans to the saucepan and quickly stir, coating them as the liquid evaporates. Turn the heat down and then off when all liquid has disappeared.
4. Add the sugar mixture and toss until pecans are well coated.

Serves: 6-8

Lori Russell
"It takes almost no time to make these and they work at almost any function, casual or formal."

Jazzy Chicken Salad

1/2 lb sliced bacon
3/4 cup mayonnaise
1 tsp salt
1/4 tsp pepper
1 cup croutons
3 cups cooked, diced, white meat chicken
2 tomatoes, sliced and quartered
1 tbsp Worcestershire sauce
1 tbsp minced parsley
1 tbsp minced scallions or chives
1 tbsp capers

1. Cook bacon until crisp; break into small pieces.
2. Mix together mayonnaise, salt and pepper.
3. Combine with other ingredients. Chill and serve on bed of lettuce.
   Serves: 4

Ann Clark

Lemon and Artichoke Salad

1-2 thick skinned lemons
2 large cans artichokes, rinsed and drained
sea salt & pepper
3/4 cup almonds toasted
6 tbsp mild honey
juice of 1 1/2 lemons
1/3 cup extra virgin olive oil
2 tbsp fresh thyme leaves

1. Wash lemons. Cover with water in small sauce pan. Add 1-2 ounces salt. Cover with lid upside down so lemons stay below surface of water. Boil for 30 minutes; drain and cool.
2. Quarter and cut large artichoke pieces into eighths. Place in bowl and season with salt and pepper to taste.
3. Cut boiled lemons in half. Scoop out and discard pulp and inner segments. Cut soft skins into quarters or eighths. Add lemon skins and almonds to artichoke hearts.
4. Mix honey with lemon juice. Add olive oil, season with salt and pepper. Pour over artichokes and stir in thyme to taste.
   Serves: 6

Sanne Kure-Jensen

"Widely loved by adult dinner guests."

Spicy Super Crunchy Fried Chicken

1 whole chicken cut into pieces or 8-10 leg
    quarters and thighs
1 tbsp curry powder
1/2 tsp ground allspice
2 tbsp garlic, minced
salt and pepper to taste
1 Scotch bonnet (habenero) pepper or other
    fresh chili, seeded, minced
1 egg
2 tbsp water
1 cup flour
canola or vegetable oil
lemon or lime for garnish

1. In a bowl, combine curry, allspice, garlic, salt, pepper, chili pepper, egg and water. Toss in chicken to coat.
2. By hand, blend tossed chicken with flour until coated (adjusting water and/or flour as needed). Chicken should remain dry but not powdery. Note: you may refrigerate chicken for up to 24 hours if needed.
3. Choose a skillet or casserole at least 12-inches in diameter that can be covered. Add enough oil to come to a depth of about 1/2-inch and turn heat to medium-high. When oil is hot, raise heat.
4. Slowly add chicken pieces to skillet. Cover skillet, reduce heat to medium-high and cook for 7 minutes; cook uncovered for another 7 minutes. Turn chicken again and cook for about 5 minutes more, turning to ensure all sides are brown.
5. Remove chicken from skillet and drain on paper towels. Serve at any temperature with lemon or lime wedges.

Serves: 4

Kathleen Beckett

The Best Ribs Ever

Ribs:
3 racks of baby back ribs
1 tbsp salt
2 tbsp mixed pickling spices
1 medium onion, sliced

Sauce:
1/2 cup barbeque sauce (Bullseye Original)
1/4 cup dark corn syrup

1. Cut racks of ribs in half. Place ribs in large pan and cover with water. Add salt, pickling spices and onion slices.
2. Heat to a boil then lower heat. Cover and simmer ribs for one hour. Remove ribs from water and let cool.
3. When ready to grill ribs, coat them with the sauce. Grill, turning and basting, until ribs are evenly glazed. Remember they are already cooked so you just need to get the sauce good and crispy.

Serves: 6

Donna Flynn

"Most people end up eating more than half a rack!"

Provencal Potato Salad

Salad:
1 lb small white boiling potatoes
1 lb small red boiling potatoes
2 tbsp dry white wine
2 tbsp chicken stock
1/2 lb haricot verts, stems removed
1/2 cup capers
1 cup halved cherry tomatoes
1/2 cup small-diced red onion
1/2 cup oil-cured black olives, pitted
1/4 cup minced scallions
2 tbsp minced fresh dill
2 tbsp minced flat-leaf parsley
2 tbsp minced fresh basil leaves

Vinaigrette:
3 tbsp white wine vinegar
1/2 tsp dijon mustard
1/2 tsp salt
1/4 tsp black pepper
1/2 cup olive oil

1. Cook potatoes in salted boiling water for 20-30 minutes, until tender. Drain and let cool. Cut potatoes in half or quarters (if larger) and place in a large bowl.
2. Add wine and chicken stock and toss gently. Allow liquids to soak into the potatoes.
3. Blanch haricot verts in salted water for 3-5 minutes. Drain and immerse in ice cold water for 5 minutes. Drain again and set aside.
3. For vinaigrette, combine vinegar, mustard, 1/2 tsp salt and 1/4 tsp pepper in a bowl. Slowly add olive oil while whisking to make an emulsion. Add the vinaigrette to the potato salad.
4. Add haricot verts and all remaining ingredients to potato salad. Combine gently. Serve at room temperature.

Serves: 6

Bethany Di Napoli

" I love to make this for family gatherings in the summer.
It is a great side dish."

A Newport Summer Moment...

"I feel that Newport Summers are very unique. From swimming at the beach to having the company of friends, there is always something to do (or not do!)! However, I have to say, that the best part of Newport summers are how laid back they are! You never feel like you MUST be doing something but there is always something you CAN do! That is why I love Newport summers."

Abby Russell (Class of 2007)

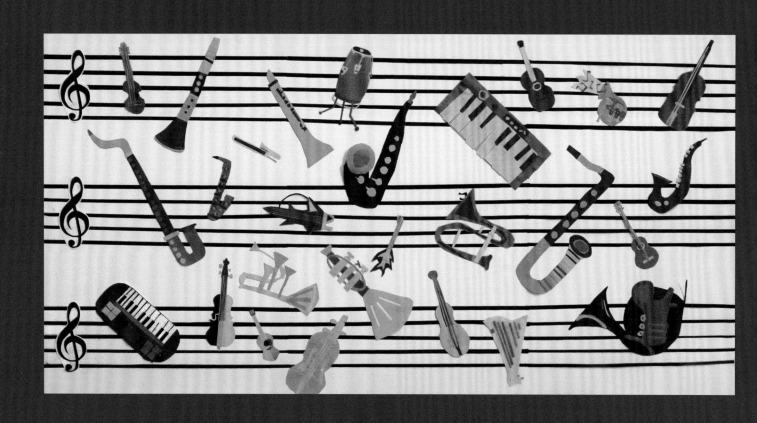

Jazz Notes

7TH GRADE, CLASS OF 2007

Nutted Wild Rice

1 cup (1/2 lb) raw wild rice
5 1/2 cups chicken stock
1 cup shelled pecan halves
1 cup yellow raisins
grated rind of 1 large orange
1/4 cup chopped fresh mint
4 scallions, thinly sliced
1/4 cup olive oil
1/3 cup fresh orange juice
1 1/2 tsp salt
ground pepper to taste

1. Put rice in a strainer and run under cold water; rinse thoroughly. Place rice in a medium-sized heavy saucepan. Add stock and bring to a rapid boil. Adjust heat to a gentle simmer and cook uncovered for 45 minutes. After 30 minutes check for doneness; rice should not be too soft.

2. Place a thin towel or cheesecloth inside a colander and turn rice into the colander and drain. Transfer drained rice to a bowl.

3. Add remaining ingredients to rice and toss gently. Adjust seasonings to taste. Let mixture stand in refrigerator for 2 hours to allow flavors to develop. Serve at room temperature.

Serves: 6

Monique Burgess

*"The mint adds an unexpected mmm... to this dish.
It's always a winner for dinner parties or pot luck."*

Microbrew Beer Bread

3 cups of self-rising flour
3 tbsp sugar
12 oz warm beer

Preheat oven to 350°.

1. Mix ingredients into a smooth batter, but do not over mix.

2. Pour batter into a well greased loaf pan. Bake for approximately 90 minutes until a knife comes out clean. Bread should be golden brown.

Note: Bread will take on the taste of the beer you select. Commercial beers will work just fine, but the flavor is weaker. For best results, use a full-bodied beer you love, i.e., Octoberfest, winter beers, fruit based, European beers, etc.

Serves: 8-10

Kimberly Lugo

"It is also great cut into chunks for dipping."

Le Bistro Newport

Creole Bread Pudding

Pudding:
2 tbsp butter
1 12 oz loaf of stale French bread
1 qt milk
2 cups sugar
1/2 cup raisins
2 tbsp vanilla extract
3 eggs

Bourbon Sauce:
4 oz unsalted butter
1 cup sugar
1 egg
1/2 cup bourbon

Preheat oven to 350°.

1. Spread the butter on the inside of a 10-inch cake pan, 2- inches deep.

2. Break the bread into chunks and put into a bowl. Add milk. Crumble the bread into small pieces and let it soak until all the milk is absorbed.

3. In another bowl, beat the eggs and sugar together until thick. Add raisins and vanilla. Stir into the bread mixture and mix well.

4. Pour into the buttered cake pan and spread it out evenly. Place the cake pan into a larger pan and add boiling water to a depth of 1-inch. Bake for about 1 hour or until the pudding is set.

5. For the sauce, cut the butter into 1/2-inch pieces and melt over very low heat. Combine the sugar and the egg, and add to the melted butter. Stir over low heat until the sugar dissolves and mixture thickens. Do not allow to boil. Let it cool slightly before adding the bourbon.

Serves: 8-10

*Nothing like this sweet and creamy French Quarter dessert
to go along with some great New Orleans jazz!*

Watermelon with Mango and Lime

1 (4 lb) piece of seedless watermelon,
    cut into 1-inch chunks
2 mangoes, peeled, pitted, cut into
    1-inch chunks
1 tbsp lime juice
1 tsp finely grated lime zest
1/2 tsp sugar
ginger, grated to taste

1. Toss all ingredients together, cover and chill for 20 minutes.

2. Stir a few times while chilling.

3. Serve in fancy, stemmed, shallow glasses for fancy dinner/brunch or colorful plastic glasses for picnic.

Serves: 6

Leslie Holloway

"Guests love the fact that the dessert is light and refreshing while also tangy and sweet."

Macadamia Lime Pie

1 3.5-oz jar roasted macadamia nuts, rinsed and dried
1 cup fine vanilla wafer cookie crumbs (about 26 cookies)
1 tbsp sugar
1/2 stick butter, melted
1 cup plus 2 tbsp fresh lime juice (Key limes if possible)
1 tsp unflavored gelatin
3 egg yolks
1 14-oz can sweetened condensed milk
1 tsp grated lime zest
1 cup chilled whipping cream, whipped to stiff peaks

Preheat oven to 350°.

1. Place nuts on cookie sheet and toast until golden brown, stirring several times; about 2 minutes. Remove from oven and cool completely.
2. Grind 1 cup macadamia nuts in food processor. Transfer nuts to medium bowl. Add cookie crumbs, sugar and butter and mix. Press mixture into 9-inch pie pan. Bake about 10 minutes, until golden brown. Cool.
3. Place 2 tablespoons lime juice in small bowl. Sprinkle gelatin over and let stand until softened, about 10 minutes.
4. Meanwhile, whisk egg yolks and condensed milk in heavy medium sauce pan to blend. Whisk in remaining 1 cup lime juice. Stir over medium heat 6 minutes to cook egg yolks (do not boil). Add softened gelatin and lime zest and stir until gelatin dissolves. Pour filling into prepared crust and refrigerate until filling is set, about 6 hours or overnight.
5. Spread whipped cream over pie. Chop remaining macadamia nuts and sprinkle over whipped cream. Cut into wedges and serve.

Serves: 4-6

Allison deHorsey

Gingersnaps

1 cup sugar
3/4 cup shortening
1/3 cup dark molasses
1 egg
2 1/4 cups flour
1 1/2 tsp baking soda
1 1/2 tbsp of ginger
1 1/2 tsp of ground cinnamon
1/4 tsp salt
sugar for coating

Preheat oven to 375°.

1. Mix sugar, shortening, molasses and egg.
2. In a second bowl, combine flour, baking soda, ginger, cinnamon, and salt. Gradually blend the flour mixture into the creamed mixture with an electric mixer. Cover and refrigerate a minimum of one hour.
3. Roll dough into small balls and roll in sugar to coat completely. Place about 1-2 inches apart on a cookie sheet and bake 8-10 minutes. Let stand for 2 minutes on cookie sheet. Cool on a wire rack..

Serves: 12

Kimberly Lugo

Turtle Bars

1 box of dark chocolate cake mix
1/2 cup butter melted
2/3 cup of evaporated milk
14 oz package of light caramels
12 oz package of semi-sweet
   chocolate morsels
1 cup coarsely chopped pecans

Preheat oven to 350°.

1. Place cake mix, melted butter and 1/3 cup of evaporated milk in mixing bowl and beat.
2. Place 1/2 cake mixture in a greased 9 x 13 inch pan. Press evenly into bottom of pan. Bake for 6 minutes. Remove from oven and cool to room temperature.
3. Place caramels and 1/3 cup evaporated milk in a sauce pan and stir over medium heat until smooth.
4. Pour evenly over baked cake, spread with spatula.
5. Sprinkle chocolate morsels and nuts evenly across the top of caramel topping. Spread the rest of the cake mixture on top of the morsels and nuts.
6. Bake 15-18 minutes. Cool and cut into desired squares.
   Serves: 8

Tony Raitano and Sheila Connery

Lemonade by the Sea

1 1/2 cups freshly squeezed lemon
   juice (from about 12 lemons)
1/2 cup sugar
1 cup water
2 6-oz. cans of pineapple juice
1 12-oz. can apricot nectar
2 12-oz. cans ginger ale

1. Combine all ingredients and stir until sugar dissolves.
2. Add 5 more cups of water and mix well .
3. Chill until cold. Serve with a few slices of lemons to garnish and plenty of ice.
   Yield: 1 pitcher

Krista Peterson

"Kids love this too!"

4th of July Cookout

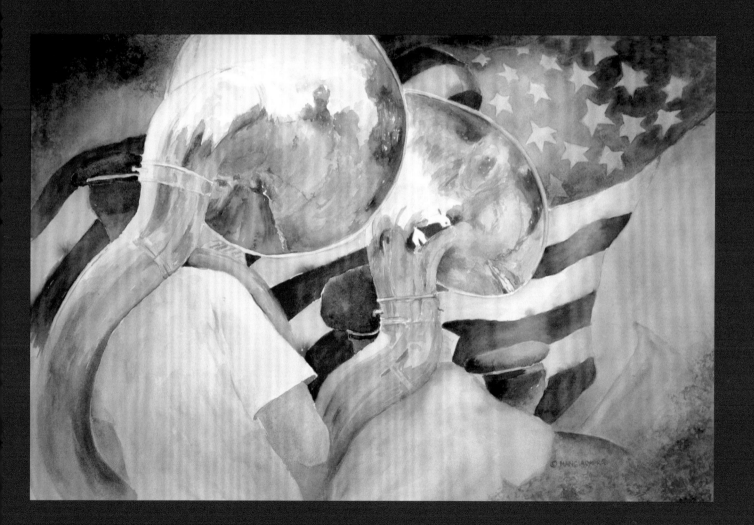

4th of July

Day and night, enjoy events in Newport that will make you "Proud to be an American" on this 4th of July holiday. Independence Day celebrations abound. Head to Bristol, 15 miles north of Newport, for the Annual Fourth of July Celebration and parade which was established in 1785 and is the oldest continuous celebration of its kind in the United States. For a concert and fireworks at Dewey Field, Naval Station Newport, bring your lawn chairs and blankets, and relax on the lawn overlooking Newport Harbor, and watch the fireworks dance over your head. Or, plan on attending the fireworks salute from Fort Adams. Happy 4th!

About the Artist

Paola Mangiacapra, "Bristol 4th of July"

Paola Mangiacapra is a retired public school teacher who has been painting in watercolor for thirteen years. She has studied with and been inspired by locally and nationally prominent artists who have helped to shape her vision as she develops a strong, expressive approach in handling watercolor. She aspires to transform ordinary scenes or subject matter into extraordinary images through design, color, and the fluidity of the medium.

She is an artist member of the Catherine Lorillard Wolfe Art Club and the Rhode Island Watercolor Society and is a signature member of the Northeast Watercolor Society. Her work appears frequently in juried shows throughout the Northeast and is often recognized with awards. Paola's studio is in West Kingston, Rhode Island, and her paintings can be found in Newport at Spring Bull Gallery.

4th of July Cookout

Menu Selections

Chilled Gazpacho

Portuguese Littlenecks

Spinach Salad with Warm Bacon, Mushrooms and Citrus Compote

Grilled Ginger and Peppercorn Flank Steak
Kobe Beef Burger
Barbecue Chicken
Grilled Shrimp with Scallops over Wilted Baby Spinach
with a Sweet Corn & Basil Coulis
Grilled Striped Bass with Corn, Tomatoes, and Green Beans

Grilled Summer Squash
Corn Salad
Zucchini Tomatoes Sauté
Basil Summer Pasta

Heaven Cream
Fresh Blueberry Pie
Incredible Edibles
Strawberries with Strawberry Sauce over Ice Cream

Homemade Pink Lemonade

Clarke Cooke House

Chilled Gazpacho

1 1/2 red peppers
1 1/2 yellow peppers
1 1/2 cucumbers, peeled
1/2 jalapeño pepper, finely diced
1/4 bunch cilantro, finely chopped
1 tbsp garlic, finely minced
69 oz (8 1/2 cups) bottled
    tomato juice
1 1/2 lbs. canned whole
    tomatoes, pulsed in a food
    processor
2 tbsp extra virgin olive oil
2 tbsp sugar
1/2 cup cider vinegar
kosher salt to taste
freshly ground pepper to taste

1. Wash all vegetables well. Seed and dice peppers and cucumber to 1/4-inch. Be certain that the ribs are removed from the peppers. Place into a large stock pot.
2. Pour tomato juice and processed tomatoes into the stock pot.
3. Add olive oil, sugar, and cider vinegar. Thoroughly mix together all ingredients. Season with salt and pepper.
4. Chill. Serve in a cup or bowl. At the Clarke Cooke House, the gazpacho is garnished with a teaspoon of extra virgin olive oil and some chopped chives.
   Serves: 10-12

Ted Gidley, the executive chef at the Clarke Cooke House, generously shares this famous gazpacho recipe. These fresh flavors should evoke the summer scene down on the wharf, sun shining, and music drifting...

Brick Alley Pub

Portuguese Littlenecks

1 dozen fresh littlenecks
1/2 stick butter
1 tbsp garlic, chopped
12 slices chourico, skinned
1/2 tsp crushed red pepper
1/4 cup white wine
1/2 tsp black pepper
1/2 yellow onion, julienned
1 green pepper, julienned
2 tbsp fresh cilantro
4 tbsp red pepper, chopped

1. Put all ingredients, except the littlenecks, cilantro, and chopped red pepper, into a medium sized pot filled with water. Bring to a boil and add littlenecks.
2. Simmer for about 12-15 minutes. Remove littlenecks with a slotted spoon.
3. Serve in a deep soup bowl. Garnish with fresh cilantro and chopped red pepper. Serve with crusty Italian bread.
   Serves: 2

Truly a Rhode Island summer favorite and nobody does it better than the Brick Alley Pub.

Spinach Salad

with Warm Bacon, Mushroom and Citrus Compote

4 oz fresh domestic mushrooms,
   quartered
2 tbsp canola oil
4 oz Applewood smoked bacon
1 oz or 1/8 cup julenned red onions
1/2 cup sugar
2/3 cup champagne vinegar
1/2 cup fresh orange juice
6 oz fresh baby spinach
2 oz feta cheese
4 oz smoked salmon

1. Place bacon, mushrooms, onions and oil in a small saucepan over medium heat. Cook until bacon is golden brown.
2. Reduce heat to low. Add vinegar, sugar, and orange juice and cook for 5 minutes.
3. In a serving bowl, mix spinach, smoked salmon and feta cheese. Ladle compote over salad and serve.

Serves: 2

Grilled Ginger and Peppercorn Flank Steak

3 1/2 lb flank steak
1/4 cup light soy sauce
3/4 cup rice wine vinegar
1 tbsp garlic, chopped
1 tbsp Worcestershire sauce
1/2 cup canola oil
1 tbsp Dijon mustard
3 tbsp Asian sesame oil
1 tbsp fresh ginger, minced
1/2 cup scallions, chopped
1 tbsp peppercorns
3 tbsp molasses
3 tbsp honey
1 tbsp hot sauce
1 tsp cayenne pepper

1. Pierce flank steaks with fork.
2. Blend all remaining ingredients with a whisk, including whole peppercorns. Place steak in marinade, cover and refrigerate overnight.
3. Grill to your liking. Garnish with arugula or other seasonal herb.

Serves: 8

Lisa Davis

Kobe Beef Burger

5 lbs brisket

Brisket Rub: (enough for 2 briskets)
3/4 cup kosher salt
1/2 cup brown sugar
3 tbsp smoked Hungarian paprika

Tomato-Onion Jam:
1 large red onion, halved and sliced thin
2 tbsp olive oil
1 pint of cherry tomatoes, halved
1/4 cup red wine vinegar
1/4 cup brown sugar

Southern Slaw:
1/2 head savoy cabbage
1/2 head red cabbage
2 carrots
1 red pepper
1 green pepper

Dressing:
2 tbsp white vinegar
1 tbsp Sri Lanka curry powder
1/4 cup honey
1/4 cup Dijon mustard
2/3 cup mayonnaise
salt and pepper to taste

8 6-oz Kobe ground beef patties
8 brioche or hamburger buns

Preheat oven to 475°.

1. Brisket Preparation: Season brisket with salt and pepper. In a large roasting pan, sear brisket for good color and caramelization. Let cool enough to handle and then apply brisket rub liberally. Cover with foil and let cook in oven for 30 minutes. Reduce temperature to 350° and cook for additional 2 1/2 hours. Remove foil for last 45 minutes. If it looks dry, add a little water to roasting pan.

2. Tomato-Onion Jam: Sauté onions in olive oil. Add brown sugar and vinegar. Let simmer until liquids reduce. Add tomatoes and cook briefly so tomatoes keep their shape.

3. Southern Slaw: Slice cabbages, carrots and peppers into very thin strips. Combine all dressing ingredients together in a separate bowl and mix well. Add dressing to slaw and mix to coat well.

4. To serve: Grill burgers to desired doneness and toast buns. Place burger on bun. Shred the brisket, it should fall apart fairly easily, and place 1/2 cup on top of each burger. Spread tomato onion jam, then slaw and top with the bun. Enjoy!

Serves: 8 (Note: trimmings will serve 12)

"The Kobe Beef Burger is a favorite at the Spiced Pear and was voted by "GQ" magazine to be out of 20, the best burger to eat before you die. It is found on our private dining, lunch, and bar menus."

Barbecued Chicken

2 broiling chickens, cut into
  quarters, or 8 chicken breast halves

Sauce:
1/4 cup packed brown sugar
1/4 cup Dijon mustard
3/4 cup cider vinegar
1/2 cup pineapple or orange juice
1/4 cup Worcestershire sauce
1/2 tsp Tabasco sauce

1. Wash chicken pieces in cold water and pat dry. Place in a large, low sided glass baking dish and refrigerate while you make the sauce.
2. Place all the ingredients for the sauce in a small bowl and whisk together until well blended. Pour the sauce over the chicken and turn each piece so it is coated with barbecue sauce.
3. Cover the pan with plastic wrap and refrigerate for several hours. Remove the chicken from the refrigerator an hour before cooking, turn the pieces again, and let them sit out at room temperature.
4. Preheat a gas grill or build a charcoal fire while the chicken sits at room temperature. Turn the gas grill to low or spread out the coals to provide a low even heat. Remove the chicken from the dish and place the pieces on the grill. With a pastry brush, brush each piece with the barbecue sauce and reserve the remaining sauce. Turn each piece and brush again. Close the lid of the gas grill and cook the chicken for 50 to 60 minutes or until crusty and tender. Brush with the sauce every 15 minutes. Remove the chicken from the grill and place on a serving dish.
    Serves: 8

Lloyd Kinnear

A Newport Summer Moment...
"Every year we go with special friends and neighbors to Fort Adams for July 4th
fireworks. Lying out on the lawn only a few hundred feet from the harbor and just another short
distance from the floating pyrotechnic launch pad, drinking champagne and watching one of the
finest commemorations of our country's independence — in one of the forts that was operational
at the time we actually gained freedom — makes for an incredibly strong connection to our past.
And it galvanizes my awareness that Newport is one of the truly great cities in America today."
—Richard Zienowicz

4th of July Celebration

Grilled Shrimp and Scallops over Wilted Baby Spinach

with a Sweet Corn and Basil Coulis

Sauce:
4 tsp shallots, chopped
1 clove garlic, chopped
1/4 cup olive oil
4 cups corn, frozen
1 1/2 tbsp fresh basil, chopped
1 tsp salt
1/2 tsp white pepper
3 cups heavy cream

Seafood:
12 jumbo shrimp, peeled, deveined
    and butterflied
16 large sea scallops
salt and pepper to taste
1 tbsp garlic powder
3 tbsp olive oil
1 1/2 lbs baby spinach
fresh chives for garnish

Sauce:
1. In a saucepan, sauté chopped garlic and shallots in olive oil over medium heat.
2. Add basil and corn to the saucepan and continue to sauté for 2 minutes.
3. Add seasonings and heavy cream and let simmer for 5 minutes.
4. Puree mixture in a blender. (Be very careful; do this in small batches to ensure you do not burn yourself.)

Seafood:
1. Season the shrimp and scallops with salt, pepper, garlic powder, and a drizzle of olive oil.
2. Place shrimp on a hot grill and cook until completely cooked through.

Finish:
1. Heat 3 tablespoons olive oil in a large skillet over high heat. Add spinach and toss in the oil 1 to 2 minutes or just until wilted. Remove spinach from the skillet immediately or it will overcook. Salt and pepper to taste.
2. Place the spinach in the middle of a plate and pour the sauce around the spinach.
3. Place the grilled seafood around the spinach, reserving 1 scallop for top of each dish.
4. Garnish with two chive sprigs, per plate.

Serves: 4

22 Bowen's is known for their exquisite food and unbeatable scene.
This perfect dish will not disappoint.

Grilled Striped Bass
with Corn, Tomatoes, and Green Beans

Vinaigrette:
1 lime, zested
1 lemon, zested
3 tbsp lime juice
1/4 cup lemon juice
1 shallot, finely chopped
Pinch of red pepper flakes
2 tsp Dijon mustard
3/4 cup extra virgin olive oil
salt and freshly ground pepper to
    taste

Bass and Vegetables:
1-1/2 cups haricots verts,
    cut in 2-inch pieces
6 ears of corn, shucked
2 tbsp butter
6 8-oz striped bass fillets
salt and freshly ground pepper
2 tbsp crushed coriander seeds
4 scallions, chopped
1 small Bermuda onion, diced
4 medium tomatoes,
    cut into wedges
1/2 cup fresh basil leaves, shredded
4 tbsp blended oils
handful of parsley

1. *Vinaigrette:* Combine all ingredients, except the oil. Then, whisk in the oil slowly and season with salt and pepper.

2. *Vegetables:* Blanch beans in rapidly boiling salted water until slightly crisp. Drain beans in a colander and refresh in ice to stop the cooking and retain the color. Cut corn kernels off the cobs. Sauté the corn kernels in a large skillet with the butter, until just barely done. Season carefully with salt and pepper.

3. *Corn Stock:* Break each (now naked) cob in half and place in a large sauce pan. Add water to cover and simmer for 30 minutes. Remove the cobs, strain the liquid into another pan and boil to reduce to 1/3 cup. Set corn stock aside.

4. *Bass:* Season both sides of the bass fillets with kosher salt, pepper and coriander seed. Lightly coat with olive oil. Cook the fillets over a medium hot fire on the grill. Be sure to take them off just before they are cooked through, as they will continue to cook for a minute or two after they have been removed.

Finish: While the fillets are on the grill, pour the reduced corn stock into a large skillet. Add the corn and the cooked beans. Gently reheat. Then, remove from heat and add scallions, tomatoes, diced Bermuda onion, and vinaigrette. Toss together and check seasoning. Divide the corn mixture on individual plates and place the bass on top. Garnish with chopped parsley.

Serves: 6

John Philcox, chef extraordinaire at Café Zelda, has shared this fantastic recipe
that embodies the flavors of summer and is easily made ahead.
What sun-loving chef wouldn't love that feature?

Grilled Summer Squash

1/4 cup fresh lemon juice
1/4 cup plain yogurt
1 tbsp olive oil
2 tsp chopped fresh rosemary
1/2 tsp freshly ground black pepper
2 garlic cloves, minced
3/4 tsp salt, divided
3 small yellow squash, halved
    lengthwise
3 small zucchini, halved lengthwise
cooking spray

Prepare grill.
1. Combine the first 6 ingredients in a 13 x 9 inch baking dish. Add 1/2 teaspoon salt.
2. Make diagonal cuts, 1/4-inch deep, across cut side of each squash and zucchini half. Place squash and zucchini halves, cut sides down in baking dish. Marinate squash and zucchini at room temperature for 15 minutes.
3. Remove squash and zucchini from marinade and discard marinade. Place squash and zucchini on grill rack coated with cooking spray. Grill 5 minutes on each side or until tender. Sprinkle evenly with 1/4 teaspoon of salt.
Serves 6

Krista Peterson

Corn Salad

Vinaigrette:
1 bunch cilantro, washed and
    stemmed
1/2 cup lime (or lemon) juice
1/2 cup olive oil
salt and pepper to taste
1 garlic head
1/4 cup red onion

Salad:
2-3 red peppers, cored and diced
1 yellow pepper, cored and diced
10 ears corn, cooked, kernels
    removed
Optional:
1 12-ounce can kidney beans, drained
jalapeno pepper, finely chopped to
    taste

1. In a food processor, combine cilantro, lime juice, olive oil, salt and pepper. Blend until smooth and cilantro is finely chopped.
2. Add garlic and onion, blend until onion finely processed.
3. In a large bowl, mix peppers, corn, kidney beans (optional) and jalapeno (optional). Add the vinaigrette and mix carefully. Refrigerate before serving.
Serves: 8-10

Allison deHorsey

Zucchini Tomatoes Sauté

1 onion, finely chopped
2 tbsp olive oil
1 clove garlic, minced or pressed
2 medium tomatoes, peeled,
    chopped
1/2 tsp salt
1 tbsp fresh basil, chopped or
    1/2 tsp dried
1/4 tsp sugar
1/4 tsp oregano
dash pepper
1/4 cup dry white wine
    or chicken broth
1 1/2 lbs zucchini (4-6 medium),
    unpeeled, sliced 1/4 inch thick

1. Heat oil and cook onion in a large frying pan until soft but not browned. Mix in garlic, tomatoes, salt, basil, sugar, oregano, pepper and wine.
2. Bring to boiling. Cover and reduce heat. Simmer for 20 minutes.
3. Uncover and mix in zucchini. Cook over medium-high heat, stirring frequently, until tomato sauce is reduced and thickened and zucchini is tender-crisp, about 8 minutes. Salt to taste.
    Serves: 6-8

Anna Kyriakides

*"This vegetable side dish can also be served as a quick sauce for pasta
with lots of freshly grated Parmesan cheese."*

Basil Summer Pasta

3-4 large ripe tomatoes, cut into
    1/2-inch dice
1 lb Brie, rind removed, torn into
    irregular pieces
1 cup fresh basil leaves, julienne
3 garlic cloves, finely minced
1 cup extra virgin olive oil
1/2 tsp salt
1/2 tsp pepper
1 1/2 lbs linguini

1. Combine tomatoes, brie, basil, garlic, salt, pepper and olive oil in a large bowl.
2. Cover at room temperature for a minimum of 2 hours before serving.
3. Cook pasta; drain and toss with the tomato mixture.
    Serves: 4-6

Johna Toppa

"This recipe is easy and nice to prepare ahead of time."

Heaven Cream

4 egg yolks
1/2 cup sugar
1 tsp cornstarch
7 oz whipping cream, heated gently
4 oz rum
8 oz cream cheese, at room
    temperature

1. In heavy saucepan, beat yolks and sugar with wire whisk until thick. Add cornstarch; slowly stir in hot whipping cream.
2. Place mixture over medium heat, stir with wooden spoon to just below simmer.
3. Remove from heat, add half of the rum. Cool completely.
4. Whip cream cheese into it, beat the cooled custard. Add remaining rum.
5. Cover and place in refrigerator for 4 hours or overnight.
6. To serve, spoon cream into individual serving dishes and cover with fresh whole strawberries, raspberries, blueberries or peaches.

Serves: 8-10

Jane Hence

"There is never even the tiniest bit left in anyone's dish. This is deceiving, it's easy to make, sounds rather ordinary and unexciting, but it's delicious and looks beautiful."

Fresh Blueberry Pie

2 1/2 cups fresh blueberries
    (heaping cups)
1 cup sugar
1/4 cup flour
1/8 tsp salt
2 tbsp butter
pastry for bottom and top crust

Preheat oven to 400°.
1. Combine blueberries, sugar, flour and salt.
2. Pour berry mixture into an 8 inch pastry lined pie pan. Dot with butter and adjust top crust.
3. Bake for 15 minutes, then reduce heat to 325° and bake for 1 hour and 30 minutes.

Serves: 6-8

Tamara Farrick

"Buy fresh blueberries from the Farmer's Market on Pelham or by Chaves in Middletown. The filling can be thrown together in 5 minutes. Serve warm with vanilla ice cream."

Incredible Edibles

3/4 cup melted margarine
2 cups graham cracker crumbs
1 1/2 cups peanut butter
2 cups confectioners sugar
12 oz chocolate bits

1. Mix first 4 ingredients together and beat with a wooden spoon or mixer until crumbly. Put in 9 x 13 inch ungreased pan.
2. Melt chocolate in microwave; spread it over peanut butter mixture.
3. Let stand until chocolate hardens. Cut into bars.

Serves: 8

Claire Stieff

"These taste like Reese's Cups. Kids love 'em."

Strawberries with Strawberry Sauce over Ice Cream

Sauce:
1 pint fresh strawberries
2-3 tbsp sugar
2 tbsp strawberry liqueur

2 pints fresh strawberries, sliced
1 half gallon vanilla ice cream

1. To make sauce: puree strawberries, sugar, and liqueur in blender.
2. Scoop ice cream into serving dishes.
3. Top with fresh, sliced strawberries and drizzle with strawberry sauce. May be garnished with sprigs of fresh mint. Serve immediately.

Serves: 6

Nancy Estrada

"Although very simple, this looks great and tastes delicious."

Homemade Pink Lemonade

2 lemons
2 cups cold water
6-8 strawberries, cleaned and hulled
4 tsp sugar

1. Cut the lemons in half, squeeze them over a bowl.
2. Pour lemon juice, minus any seeds, into a blender, add strawberries and blend.
3. Add water and sugar and mix well.
4. Pour into glasses and add ice.

Serves: 4

Bonnie Weber

Tailgate at the Polo Match

Newport International Polo Series

Experience one of the best-kept secrets of a Newport summer: The Newport International Polo Series. It is one of Newport's oldest traditions, dating back to the 1876 founding of the first polo club in America in this seaside resort. The series features international rivals playing against USA. Polo is held every Saturday afternoon from June through September. The polo fields of Glen Farm are in Portsmouth, RI, just six miles north of downtown Newport. Pack your picnic basket and coolers, park your car within feet of the polo field, and feel the excitement of this classic sport.

About the Artist

Ray Caram, "American Championship Classic"

Ray Caram worked with major corporations based in New York City for much of his career. It was in New York City that he was requested to paint the origins of the Seven Major Professional Sports. These paintings now hang in their respective Sports Halls of Fame, including the Newport Tennis Hall of Fame.

Next came the commission to paint the 13 major winter events for the leading sponsor of the 1980 Olympics. These paintings hang in the National Art Museum of Sports in Silvermine, Connecticut, and in the Olympic Headquarters in Colorado. As a result of these paintings, he was chosen in 1982 by the U.S. Postal Service to design and paint 24 national stamps of the 1984 Olympics.

Ray was later commissioned to create 3 paintings promoting the Ralph Lauren Polo line. Then, after moving to Rhode Island, he traveled to Greenwich, Connecticut, to see the American Cadillac Polo Championships. From that visit came the inspiration for this painting, "American Championship Classic." Ray lives in Newport and his paintings can be found at the Spring Bull Gallery in Newport.

Tailgate at the Polo Match

MENU SELECTIONS

Fresh Tomato Salsa
Gi-Gi's Crab Cakes
Gruyere and Parmesan Croustillants with Lavender Salt
Spicy Black Bean Salsa

❧

Roasted Green Bean, Red Onion and Beet Salad
Cold Beef Salad Vinaigrette

❧

Spinach Lasagna Special
Nutty Cucumber Sandwich
Lemon Chicken

❧

Pesto Green Beans with Three Types of Tomatoes
Carrots with Minted Mustard Vinaigrette
Grilled Baby Eggplant with Red Pepper Sauce

❧

Great Grandma's Boston Creams
Banana Split Cake
Lemon Bars

Fresh Tomato Salsa

1 1/2 cups fresh tomatoes, peeled, chopped
1/2 cup red onion, finely chopped
1/4 cup mild or hot chili pepper, finely minced
2 tbsp garlic, minced
1/4 cup fresh cilantro, chopped

1. Combine all ingredients.
2. Let stand about 1 hour to blend flavors.
3. Use same day it is made. Serve with chili, corn chips, grilled fish, etc.

Serves: 4-6

Tom Paterson

Gi-Gi's Crab Cakes

1 lb jumbo lump crabmeat
1/4 cup mayonnaise
1 egg
1 tsp water
1/2 cup seasoned breadcrumbs
1/2 tsp lemon juice
3 sprigs parsley, chopped
dash of Worcestershire sauce
dash salt and pepper

Preheat broiler on high.
1. Put crabmeat in large bowl. Add mayonnaise, egg and water, and lightly stir.
2. Add seasoned breadcrumbs, lemon juice, parsley, Worcestershire sauce, salt and pepper to bowl. Toss lightly with fork, do not mash.
3. Form into patties. Place patties on non-stick cookie sheet.
4. Broil until browned. Flip over onto other side and broil until browned. Remove from broiler and serve with sides of cocktail sauce, tartar sauce, and lemons.

Serves: 4

Greer Beecroft

"Maryland's best!"

A Newport Summer Moment...
"Our favorite nights in Newport are done down at the beach. We join the family for appetizers, dinner, and dessert while watching the sunset."
-Marianne Menas

Gruyere and Parmesan Croustillants with Lavender Salt

8 oz Gruyere cheese, shredded
2 oz Parmesan cheese, shredded
3/4 cup butter, salted
1/2 cup plus 2 tbsp flour
pinch of cayenne pepper
3 tbsp chives, chopped
pinch of lavender salt

Preheat oven to 350°.

1. In a food processor fitted with the steel blade, combine cheeses, butter, flour and cayenne. Process for 40 - 60 seconds, just until it forms a crumbly dough.
2. Remove the dough from the processor and using your hands, form the dough into a log shape, 2-inch in diameter. Refrigerate for at least one hour.
3. Once the dough is chilled and firm, cut into 1/4-inch thick disks. Sprinkle with chives and very coarse lavender salt. Transfer to a baking sheet and bake for 10 -15 minutes, until lightly browned.

Yield: 18 biscuits

John Philcox, chef extraordinaire at Café Zelda has shared this fantastic recipe for savory and salty cheese biscuits - great with cocktails. He suggests preparing the log of dough ahead of time and keeping it in the refrigerator for up to a week, ready to bake at a moment's notice.

Spicy Black Bean Salsa

2 cans black beans
1 1/2 cups fresh corn, cooked or
   1 large can whole kernel corn,
   drained
1/2 cup or more fresh cilantro,
   chopped
6 tbsp lime juice
6 tbsp vegetable oil
1/2 cup or more red onion, finely
   chopped
1 1/2 tsp ground cumin
1 jar of your favorite hot salsa

1. Wash and drain beans.
2. Combine ingredients in a large bowl.
3. Cover and refrigerate overnight, stirring occasionally. Serve with tortilla chips.

Serves: 6-8

Roselyn Morris

"Delicious!"

Roasted Green Bean, Red Onion, and Beet Salad

10 large beets, trimmed
6 tbsp extra-virgin olive oil
8 tsp chopped fresh thyme
cooking oil spray
4 red onions, each cut into 6 wedges
2 1/2 lbs slender green beans,
    trimmed, cut into 3-inch lengths
1/4 cup water
3 tbsp balsamic vinegar
salt and pepper

Preheat oven to 400°.

1. Wrap beets tightly in foil. Place directly on oven rack. Roast until tender when pierced with knife, about 1 hour. Let cool and then peel and quarter beets. Transfer to large bowl. Add 2 tablespoons olive oil, 2 teaspoons thyme, salt, and pepper; toss to coat.

2. Spray 2 large rimmed baking sheets with nonstick spray. Divide onion wedges between prepared baking sheets. Brush onions on both sides with 2 tablespoons oil; sprinkle with 4 teaspoons thyme, salt, and pepper. Arrange onions cut side down and roast until golden brown on bottom, about 10 minutes. Turn onions over. Roast until golden brown and tender, about 10 minutes longer. Transfer to another large bowl.

3. Divide green beans between same baking sheets. Drizzle beans with remaining 2 tablespoons olive oil, water, and 2 teaspoons thyme. Sprinkle with salt and pepper. Cover tightly with foil and roast until almost crisp-tender, about 14 minutes. Uncover and continue to roast until water evaporates and beans are crisp-tender, about 5 minutes. Let cool and then transfer to bowl with onions. Let stand at room temperature.

Serves: 10

Bethany Di Napoli

A *N*ewport Summer Moment...

"Our favorite thing to do together as a family in the summer is to go to Polo on Saturday afternoons. We make a picnic supper, watch the match, visit with friends, and play soccer and Bocci in the field afterward until the sun sets."

-Jaxson, Michael and Heather de Pinho

Cold Beef Salad Vinaigrette

1/2 cup olive oil
2 tbsp red wine vinegar
2 tsp Dijon mustard
1 large clove garlic, mashed
salt and pepper
4-5 cups cubed deli roast beef
1 green pepper, finely chopped
1/2 cup minced scallions
1/2 cup minced pimento
1/2 cup green olives, halved
2 small dill gherkins, finely minced
2 tbsp capers, drained well
1/2 cup green peas, cooked
2 tbsp minced parsley
tomato wedges for garnish

1. Prepare vinaigrette by whisking first five ingredients together until smooth.
2. Combine rest of salad with dressing. Let stand in a cool place for 2-4 hours. If refrigerated, bring back to room temperature before serving.
3. Garnish with tomato wedges.

Serves: 4

Gail Ruggieri

"Ask the deli to slice the roast beef very thick and you can cube it at home. This combination of ingredients sounds odd but is really a wonderful summer salad."

Spinach Lasagna Special

1 lb lasagna noodles (about 12 noodles)
2-3 tbsp olive oil
2 cloves garlic, minced
1 medium onion, chopped
2 tomatoes, chopped
10 medium mushrooms, sliced
1/4 tsp each: dried oregano, basil and rosemary
2 tbsp fresh parsley
1 lb baby spinach, washed
1 cup low-fat cottage cheese
1/4 cup grated Parmesan cheese
16 oz grated mozzarella cheese
26 oz marinara sauce

Preheat oven 350°.
1. Cook noodles until al dente. Drain and set aside.
2. Heat oil over medium heat. Sauté garlic, onions, tomatoes and mushrooms. When onion is translucent, add herbs and spinach, stirring until spinach is wilted. Reduce to low heat and simmer for 4-5 minutes.
3. Place 1 cup mozzarella cheese aside. Combine remaining mozzarella and cottage cheese. Mix vegetables into cheese mixture thoroughly.
4. Layer noodles and vegetable-cheese mixture with marinara sauce in 8 x 13 inch baking pan. Top with reserved mozzarella and Parmesan cheese, if desired.
5. Bake for 35 minutes. Let sit 5-10 minutes before serving.

Serves: 8

Lydia Babich

"This is a Girls' Night favorite. My girlfriends have asked for this recipe repeatedly. Finally took the time to write it down!"

Polo

Nutty Cucumber Sandwich

3-4 oz soft chevre goat cheese
1/2 medium cucumber
8 thin slices rye bread
1/2 cup fresh snow pea pods,
  trimmed
1/8 cup seasoned toasted soy nuts
  (such as ranch or garlic)
1 medium tomato, thinly sliced
salt to taste

1. Slice goat cheese into four pieces and place on four slices of bread.
2. Thinly slice cucumber and place on top of goat cheese. Cover with remaining items and top with remaining bread.
3. To serve, slice with serrated knife, cutting each sandwich in half.

Serves: 4

Wendy Lambert

Lemon Chicken

2 whole chickens, 2 1/2 pounds each,
  cleansed, insides discarded, cut
  into quarters
2 cups fresh lemon juice
2 cups flour
2 tsp salt
2 tsp paprika
1 tsp ground black pepper
1/2 cup corn oil
2 tbsp grated lemon zest
1/4 cup brown sugar
1/4 cup chicken stock
1 tsp lemon extract
2 lemons sliced paper thin

1. Combine chicken pieces and lemon juice in a bowl just large enough to hold them comfortably. Cover and marinate in the refrigerator overnight, turning occasionally.
2. Drain chicken thoroughly and pat dry. Fill a plastic bag with flour, salt, paprika, and black pepper; shake well to mix. Put 2 pieces of chicken into the bag at a time and shake, coating completely.
3. Preheat oven to 350°.
4. Heat corn oil in a frying pan or cast iron Dutch oven until hot and fry chicken pieces, a few at a time, until well browned and crisp. This will take about 10 minutes per batch.
5. Arrange browned chicken in a single layer in a large shallow baking pan. Sprinkle evenly with lemon zest and brown sugar. Mix chicken stock and lemon extract together and pour around chicken pieces. Set a thin lemon slice on top of each piece of chicken. Bake for 35-40 minutes, or until tender.

Serves: 6

Monique Burgess
"This chicken has a crisp golden crust and the zing of fresh lemon. It's good hot and terrific cold. You can substitute with boneless chicken breasts in a pinch."

Pesto Green Beans with Three Types of Tomatoes

2 plum tomatoes, cored and
  quartered
1 cup yellow pear tomatoes, cut in
  half, or cherry tomatoes
1/2 cup red cherry tomatoes, cut in
  half
1/4 cup olive oil
3 garlic cloves, minced
1 1/2 lbs green beans, stem ends
  removed
1 cup pesto
1 cup grated Parmesan cheese
salt and freshly ground pepper to
  taste
1/4 cup pine nuts, toasted, optional
1/2 cup grated Parmesan cheese, to
  garnish, optional

Preheat oven to 400 °.

1. Toss the plum tomatoes, yellow pear tomatoes, and cherry tomatoes with the olive oil and garlic in a baking dish. Roast 20 to 25 minutes, until the tomatoes start to release their juices and begin to shrivel. Set aside to cool.

2. Meanwhile, bring a large saucepan of water to a boil, add the beans, and cook 1 to 2 minutes or until the beans are bright green and crisp-tender.

3. Drain the beans immediately and plunge them into a bowl of ice water to stop the cooking process. (Note: This helps the beans retain their bright color.) Remove the beans from the water and set aside to drain thoroughly.

4. Toss the beans with the pesto, Parmesan, and salt and pepper in a large bowl. Place the beans on a platter or individual serving plates and top with tomatoes. Garnish with toasted pine nuts and Parmesan (if desired) and serve.

   Serves: 8

Shelly Ferrall

"Great summer salad for picnics, tailgates, and outdoors. It is very easy; if you don't have time to make pesto, buy a good-quality, store-bought fresh pesto from the deli section."

Carrots with Minted Mustard Vinaigrette

6 large carrots, peeled and sliced
  1/8 inch thick
1/4 cup chopped fresh mint leaves

Vinaigrette:
1/4 cup lemon juice
2 tbsp olive oil
2 tbsp vegetable oil
1 tbsp Dijon mustard

1. Steam the carrots for 5 minutes or until crisp tender.

2. While carrots are steaming, combine vinegar, mustard, salt and pepper. Whisk in oil.

3. Mix the hot carrots in a bowl with the vinaigrette.

4. Cover the bowl and cool in the refrigerator for about 30 minutes.

5. Sprinkle the mint on the cooled carrots and serve at room temperature.

   Serves: 8

Sheila Powell

Grilled Baby Eggplant with Red Pepper Sauce

Red Pepper Sauce:
2 red bell peppers
2 tbsp extra-virgin olive oil
2 cloves garlic, peeled and crushed
1 tsp finely chopped fresh rosemary
pinch of cayenne
salt and freshly ground pepper to
     taste

Eggplant:
1 1/2 lbs Japanese or baby eggplants
     (about 5)
1 tbsp olive oil
1 tbsp finely chopped fresh thyme
1/2 tsp each salt and pepper

1. Red Pepper Sauce: Prepare a grill or preheat broiler. Grill or broil peppers, turning, until blackened and blistered on all sides, 10 to 20 minutes.
2. Place peppers in a paper bag or heavy plastic food bag and close. Let them steam for 4 to 5 minutes. Slip off skins and remove stems and seeds.
3. Transfer peppers to a blender or food processor. Add oil, garlic, rosemary and cayenne; process until smooth. Season with salt and pepper. Set aside.
4. Eggplant: Prepare a grill. Place a fine-mesh vegetable grilling rack on the grill to heat.
5. Cut each eggplant in half lengthwise, then cut crosswise into 1-inch pieces. In a large bowl, toss eggplant with oil, thyme, salt and pepper.
6. Lightly oil the rack. Grill eggplant until tender, 4 to 5 minutes per side. Arrange eggplant on a platter. Serve hot or at room temperature with red pepper sauce on the side.
          Serves: 8

Bethany Di Napoli

Great-Grandma's Boston Creams

3 cups sugar
1/2 cup whipping cream
1/2 cup light cream
3/4 cup white Karo corn syrup
2 tbsp butter
chopped walnuts (optional)
1 tsp vanilla

1. Mix all ingredients, except vanilla, in a heavy pan on medium heat. Stir often until ingredients combine. Cook until mixture reaches approximately 240° with a candy thermometer or can form a soft ball in cool water.
2. Add vanilla and handbeat with wooden spoon until mixture looks creamy and dull. Add chopped walnuts, if desired. Pour into a buttered 11 x 7 inch Pyrex dish and spread out.
3. Score piece sizes on surface of candy while still soft and press large pieces of walnut on top of each piece, if desired.
4. Cut into pieces when cooled.
          Serves: 12

Kathleen Kits van Heyningen

"Only make this on a sunny day!"

Banana Split Cake

2 cups graham cracker crumbs
1/2 cup melted butter
2 sticks of butter, softened
2 eggs
2 cups confectionary sugar
3 bananas
1 large can of crushed pineapple
1 pint whipping cream (whipped)
1 small bag of crushed walnuts
1 small jar red cherries

1. Crust: Mix graham cracker crumbs and melted butter. Press into the bottom of an 8 x 8 inch square pan.
2. Blend 2 sticks of softened butter with eggs and confectionary sugar. Beat on low with mixer. Refrigerate for 10 minutes to cool.
3. Spread pudding like mixture over crumb crust in pan.
4. Drain the pineapple, saving the juice in a bowl.
5. Slice bananas into the pineapple juice to prevent browning. Drain the bananas and arrange over filling.
6. Spread the pineapple over the bananas and top with whip cream, walnuts, then cherries.
7. Keep refrigerated until served. Double recipe for 13 x 9 inch pan.

Serves: 6

Lisa Lohrum

"This recipe was passed on by my Auntie Rosie, a childhood favorite that has worked its way into every family celebration."

Lemon Bars

Crust:
1 cup flour
1/4 cup powdered sugar
1/2 cup cold butter or margarine

Filling:
2 eggs, slightly beaten
1 cup sugar
juice and zest of 1 lemon (or 2 tablespoons lemon juice)
2 tbsp flour
1/2 tsp baking powder

Preheat oven to 350°.

1. Crust: Slice the butter into small pieces. In a large bowl, combine the flour and sugar. Cut in the butter pieces with a pastry blender or with two knives until crumbled pieces are fine.
2. Press into a well-greased, 9-inch square pan and bake for 15 minutes or until golden brown around edges.
3. Filling: In a large bowl, whisk together the eggs and sugar. Add the lemon zest and juice and beat until smooth.
4. Combine the flour and baking powder and whisk this mixture into beaten egg mixture. Pour over crust and bake another 25 minutes.
5. Cool before cutting into squares. Dust with confectioners sugar before serving.

Serves: 4-6

Beverly Little

Sunset Sail Cocktails and Hors D'oeuvres

Victoria Corey 03

Newport, the Sailing City

Certain competitions are forever associated with a special location. One sporting event gave Newport international publicity for years: The America's Cup races. The cup is named after the first yacht to win the trophy, the schooner, 'America.' The trophy remained in the hands of the U.S. from 1851 until 1983, the longest winning streak in the history of sports. Today, Newport continues to be one of the most active sailing hubs in the world. On any given summer day, the harbor is bustling with activity... fleets tacking around the buoys during a regatta; pleasure boats cruising by the lighthouse; glorious yachts and sleek racing sloops pointing up the channel. Don't miss the chance to feel the excitement of bygone races. Take a sail on scenic Narragansett Bay.

About the Artist

Victoria Corey, "Sailing Past Castle Hill"

Victoria Corey, originally of Springfield, Illinois, fell in love with art at a young age. She graduated from Oldfields School and continued on to Guilford College in North Carolina where she studied art and biology. Rhode Island is now her permanent home as well as the inspiration for her art. Tory enjoys painting with watercolors and pastels with a concentration on land and seascapes of southern New England.

Her artwork has been featured on the cover of "abc" magazine, and is currently shown in galleries and shops throughout Rhode Island. Tory illustrated "Larry the Lawnmower," a full-color, 32 page, children's book that came out in December 2004. She is currently an Artist-Member of the Wickford Art Association and is a member of the Newport Art Museum, and their Artists' Guild. Her paintings can be found in Newport at Arnold Art Gallery.

Sunset Sail Cocktails and Hors D'Oeuvres

MENU SELECTIONS

New England Corn Chowder with Lobster

❧

Summer Shrimp
Hot Lobster Dip
Gravlax
Olive- Goat Cheese Bruschetta
Guacamole, Perfected
Black Bean Fritters with a Tropical Vinaigrette
Smoked Salmon Wraps
Caponata

❧

Toblerone Chocolate Mousse
Coconut Macaroons

New England Corn Chowder with Lobster

6 oz smoked bacon
1 medium onion, diced
2 carrots, peeled and sliced
  diagonally
3 1/4 lbs red Bliss potatoes, sliced
2 stalks celery, sliced
6 ears corn, kernels removed, or 1 1/4
  pounds corn kernels
3 cups chicken stock
1 tbsp thyme
1 bay leaf
1 oz red hot sauce
1 pint milk
1 pint cream
1 tbsp sugar
1 1/2 pound lobster meat, cooked,
  and shelled
1 tomato, diced
4 tsp chives, finely
  chopped

1. In a large stock pot, sauté bacon until crispy. Add onions, carrots, potatoes and celery and continue to sauté for 3 minutes.
2. Add corn, chicken stock, thyme, bay leaf, red hot sauce, milk and cream. Simmer for 15 minutes or until vegetables are tender.
3. Puree half this mixture in a blender then add back to the other half of mixture. Season with salt, pepper and sugar.
4. Add lobster meat and warm through.
5. Ladle into soup bowls and garnish with chopped tomatoes and chives.
   Serves: 8

Yesterday's, where everyone meets, has shared its secret recipe for the eternal favorite, Corn Chowder. Enjoy!

Summer Shrimp

2 cloves garlic
1 cup oil
1/3 cup white vinegar
salt & pepper
1 cup chopped chives
1 tbsp chopped scallion
1 cup chopped parsley
1 lb of cooked shrimp, medium to
  large

Mix all ingredients and pour over shrimp. Marinade shrimp between 12-48 hours. Drain and serve with toothpicks.
   Serves: 6

Kathleen Glassie
"Always the first to go aboard our sailing cruises. Great paired with crisp Pinot Grigio."

Hot Lobster Dip

8 oz cream cheese
1/4 cup mayonnaise
1 clove garlic, minced
1 tsp grated onion
1 tsp Dijon mustard
1 tsp sugar
pinch salt
1 cup cooked lobster meat, chopped
sherry to taste

1. Melt cream cheese in saucepan over medium low heat.
2. Add mayo, garlic, onion, mustard, sugar and salt. Mix well.
3. Add lobster and sherry. Heat through. Pour into serving bowl and serve with crackers.

Serves: 4

Susan Kehoe

"A family favorite nibble at cocktail hour! It goes fast!"

Gravlax

1 cup kosher salt
1/4 cup fresh dill, chopped
1 tbsp freshly grated orange zest
1 tsp freshly grated lime zest
1/4 tsp freshly grated black pepper
4 tbsp vodka
1 4-lb side fresh salmon, skin on,
    rinsed under cold water
1/2 cup sugar

Accompaniment:
capers
finely chopped red onion
chopped fresh dill
chopped hard boiled eggs, separated
Pumpernickel bread slices, small

1. Combine the salt, dill, orange and lime zests, pepper, and vodka in a small bowl and mix thoroughly.
2. Place the salmon, skin side down, on several large sheets of plastic wrap and pack the salt-curing mixture over the entire cut of salmon. Press the mixture firmly onto the fish, wrap tightly in plastic. Put skin side up on a baking sheet and place something heavy onto the fish. Refrigerate 24-48 hours.
3. Remove salmon from the fridge and brush off the salt. Rinse thoroughly under cold water. Sprinkle the sugar all over the salmon, packing firmly with your hands. Re-wrap in plastic, place on baking sheet and refrigerate ONE WEEK.
4. To serve, thinly slice gravlax and arrange on a platter. Place small bowls on a platter filled with capers, red onion, dill, hard boiled egg whites and hard boiled egg yolks. Place small pumpernickel bread slices, toasted, on the platter as well.

Serves: 8

Shelly Ferrall & Hal Petri

"We brought this to a family picnic, expecting only adults to eat it.
How surprised we were to see 7-year-olds inhaling it! You never know!"

Sunset Sail

KINDERGARTEN, CLASS OF 2014

Olive-Goat Cheese Bruschetta

1 cup diced seeded plum tomatoes
1/4 cup chopped pitted olives
   (green Sicilian or Kalamata)
2 tbsp sherry vinegar
1/8 tsp each salt and pepper
16 slices French bread baguette
   (1/4-inch thick slices)
1 garlic clove, peeled
1/4 cup mild goat cheese at room
   temperature

Preheat oven to 400°.

1. Combine tomatoes, olives, vinegar, salt and pepper in a small bowl, and set aside.
2. Arrange bread on a baking sheet; bake for 8 minutes or until lightly browned and crisp. Remove toast slices from oven and cool 2 minutes.
3. Rub both sides of each toast slice with garlic clove. Spread goat cheese thinly on 1 side of each toast and top with the olive mixture.

Serves: 8

Diane Canepari

Guacamole, Perfected

2 ripe Haas avocados
1/4 cup red onion, minced
1/4 cup fresh cilantro, coarsely
   chopped
1 clove garlic, crushed or minced
juice of one lime
1/4 to 1/2 teaspoon salt
1/4 tsp sugar
Optional but recommended:
1 tbsp jalapeno pepper, seeded,
   minced
Optional:
1/4 tsp cumin
1/2 cup sour cream
1/2 cup mild salsa

1. Cut avocados in half, remove seed and scoop out flesh with a spoon and place in medium bowl. Mash with large fork until chunky consistency is reached. Add remaining ingredients, except sour cream and salsa, and stir to combine. Serve with tortilla chips as appetizer or topping for enchiladas or other Mexican foods.
2. If the guacamole is to be served at a party or otherwise eaten over a period of time, the top can be prevented from turning black by placing the guacamole in a serving bowl, smoothing the top, and frosting with the sour cream, then mild salsa. This is delicious and won't overpower the delicate flavors.

Serves: 4-6

Frances Regas, MD

"I grew up in Southern California and I love Mexican food—particularly Guacamole. I've been adjusting this version of it for more than a decade, but for the last 3 years or so everybody who tastes it says it's the best Guacamole they've ever had, so I am finally leaving it alone!"

Black Bean Fritters with Tropical Vinaigrette

Fritters:
1/2 red bell pepper, diced
1/2 yellow bell pepper, diced
1/2 small chayote or zucchini, diced
1 cup cooked black beans
1/2 cup cornmeal
1/2 cup flour
1/2 tsp baking powder
1 tbsp packed brown sugar
1 egg beaten
1 tbsp buttermilk
peanut oil for frying

Vinaigrette:
1 very ripe mango, peeled and seeds
    removed
1/2 cup passion fruit juice
3 tbsp lime juice
1/2 cup rice wine vinegar
1/2 to 1 cup peanut oil
2 tbsp orange juice
salt to taste
honey to taste

1. Fritters: Combine the bell peppers, chayote, beans, cornmeal, flour, baking powder, and brown sugar in a large bowl. Add the egg and buttermilk and toss lightly. Season with salt and pepper.

2. Heat about 1/4-inch of peanut oil in a heavy skillet to 350°. Drop the fritter mixture into the oil by spoonfuls. Fry 1-2 minutes per side or until golden brown. Drain on paper towels in a covered dish to keep warm. Serve with tropical vinaigrette.

3. Tropical Vinaigrette: Blend the mango, passion fruit juice, and lime juice in a blender until smooth. Add vinegar and peanut oil while the blender is slowly running.

4. Mix in orange juice, salt and honey. Store, refrigerated in an airtight container. Leftover dressing can be used over fruit salad or grilled chicken.

 Serves: 6

Frances C. Regas, MD

*"This dish could be a main course at a luncheon, an appetizer, or a side dish
for a light entrée such as grilled fish."*

A Newport Summer Moment...

"I love summers in Newport for always finding the time to let the kids scamper all over the Wave sculpture— even if it means being 10 minutes late. Listening to the buoys clang just before you fall asleep. Celebrating when Frosty Freeze opens for the season. Sailing into Mackerel Cove, anchoring for lunch and doing a sunset sail back through the harbor. Doing all these things with summer house guests who love the place as much as we do!"

-Burgess Crew

Smoked Salmon Wraps

3 tbsp cream cheese
3 soft flour tortillas
4 oz smoked salmon
1/3 cup red onion, finely chopped
1/3 cup capers, drained

1. Place 1 tablespoon of cream cheese on each tortilla and spread to cover.
2. Evenly place the smoked salmon on top of the cream cheese. Sprinkle the chopped onions and capers on top of the salmon and roll.
3. Carefully slice the roll into 1/2 inch pieces and lay on a decorative plate for serving.

Serves: 6-8

Elizabeth Gallagher

"Quick, easy, and quite pretty! Everyone loves these!"

Caponata

1 1/2 lb eggplant (1 large or 2 small)
1 tbsp salt
2 large red bell peppers
1 large onion
1 large stalk celery
1/4 cup olive oil
1/8 to 1/4 tsp dried red pepper flakes
1 14-oz can whole peeled tomatoes
2-4 large cloves garlic
2 tbsp red wine vinegar
1 tbsp sugar
8 pitted Kalamata olives, chopped
1 tbsp capers, drained

1. Rinse eggplant; cut into 3/4-inch cubes. Place in colander, sprinkle with salt and toss. Let stand and drain in sink or over bowl, tossing occasionally, 1 hour. Rinse eggplant and drain well, squeeze clean in kitchen towel to extract moisture. Reserve.
2. Core and seed bell peppers; cut into 3/4-inch chunks. Chop onion coarsely. Cut celery into 1/4-inch thick slices.
3. Heat oil in 10 inch skillet over medium-high heat. Add bell peppers, onion, celery and pepper flakes; sauté 5 minutes. Add reserved eggplant; cook over medium heat, stirring occasionally, 5 minutes longer. Remove from heat.
4. Press tomatoes and their liquid through a sieve into vegetables in skillet; discard seeds. Mince garlic; add to skillet. Stir in vinegar and sugar. Cook and stir over medium high heat 3 minutes. Remove from heat.
5. Add olives and capers to skillet. Cook over medium-low heat, stirring occasionally, until sauce is thickened, about 10 minutes. Serve hot as a vegetable side dish, or, cool to room temperature and serve on an antipasto tray.

Serves: 6-8

Nancy Estrada

Toblerone Chocolate Mousse

10 ounces milk chocolate, or white chocolate Toblerone
2 whole eggs
1 2/3 cups whipping cream

1. Melt Toblerone chocolate and set aside to cool slightly.
2. Beat eggs until fluffy. Combine chocolate and egg mixture.
3. Whip the whipping cream. Do not whip it hard, you want the mousse to be nice and fluffy. Add the whipped cream to the Toblerone mixture.
4. Put it all in a nice decorative bowl or divide it into dessert glasses and let it sit in the fridge for one night.

Serves: 6-8

Daniela Frater

"Direct from Vienna: Our tradition and all-time favorite mousse recipe."

La Farge Perry House
Coconut Macaroons

2 large eggs
2/3 cup sugar
1/4 tsp salt
1 tsp vanilla extract
7 oz shredded coconut
1 cup semi-sweet chocolate chips

Preheat oven to 350°.

1. In a mixing bowl, beat the two eggs together and gradually beat in the sugar. Add the salt and vanilla extract, mixing well.
2. Add coconut and chocolate chips and mix thoroughly.
3. Place small spoonfuls on cookie sheet lined with parchment paper and bake until cookies are browned around the edges. Turn oven off and leave for additional 5-10 minutes.
4. Slide the paper off of the sheet and let cool.

Yield: 2 dozen cookies

Midge Knerr

"I treat our guests to these cookies when they arrive. They also receive a bag of four cookies with the recipe upon departure and usually are thrilled to receive them."

The Newport Music Festival

For seventeen days in mid-July, the Newport Music Festival continues its tradition of presenting unique chamber music programs. Libraries and music centers are scoured to find interesting and often neglected pieces of music. During the festival, the Newport Mansions are transformed into elegant concert halls hosting American debuts, world-class artists and special musical events. There are over sixty concerts offered throughout the festival. Choose from a concert cruise on Narragansett Bay, a box lunch alfresco concert, twilight concerts, midnight concerts — there is something for everyone.

About the Artist

Diane Gay, "Dinner Party in Newport"
Diane Gay, a local Newport artist, is known for her powerful yet delicate images of women represented in oil and acrylics. She has two ongoing series of women. "Feminine Lines" is a series executed in simple strokes that capture a movement or moment. "Elegant Women" depicts women enjoying the various activities of their lives, whether it is in a ball gown at a formal function or sitting quietly in serenity. Recently a third series has evolved; it shows elegant party and theater scenes reminiscent of the entertaining legacy of Newport. Diane's paintings can be found in many galleries throughout New England, including the Spring Bull Gallery in Newport.

Orchestrating a Bellevue Dinner

MENU SELECTIONS

Zucchini Watercress Soup

Prosciutto and Gruyere Pinwheels
Huitres Vivarois
Tuna Tartare

Roasted Fig and Arugula Salad
Warm Heirloom Tomato and Crispy Mozzarella Salad

Lobster Fatulli
Tenderloin Stuffed with Lobster
Mid-Summer Night's Salad
Pan Seared Scallops with Orange Mascarpone Sauce
Seared Local Striped Bass with Apricot Quinoa and Mushroom Fennel Vinaigrette
Sea Salt Crusted Tuna with Shallot Cream Sauce

Grilled Asparagus with Balsamic Vinegar
Tricolor Potatoes with Pesto and Parmesan
Grilled Artichokes with Olive Oil, Lemon, and Mint
Wild Mushroom Risotto

Lemon Granita
Chocolate Decadence
Vanilla Roasted Strawberries

Zucchini Watercress Soup

4 tbsp butter
2 cups yellow onions, finely chopped
3 cups chicken stock
4 medium zucchini, chopped
1-2 bunches watercress
salt and pepper to taste
fresh lemon juice to taste
1 cup heavy cream (optional)

1. Melt butter in heavy pot. Add onions, cover and cook over low heat, stirring occasionally, until onions are tender and lightly colored, about 25 minutes.
2. Add the stock and bring to a boil. Add the zucchini to the stock, return to boil. Reduce heat, cover and simmer until zucchini are very tender, about 20 minutes.
3. Pull leaves and smaller stems off the watercress, leaving about 4 loosely packed cups, or more. Rinse well.
4. Remove soup from heat, add watercress, cover, and let stand 5 minutes.
5. Pour soup through strainer, reserving liquid, transfer the solids to a food processor. Add one cup of the cooking liquid to processor and blend until smooth. Return the pureed soup to the pot and add additional cooking liquid, about 2 cups, until soup is of desired consistency. Season to taste with salt, pepper and lemon juice. Simmer briefly to heat through, serve immediately.

Serves: 4-6

Shawen Williams

"This is a very sophisticated soup, despite its humble ingredients and simple construction.
It is light, fresh and versatile and can begin any number of menus.
I prefer it with about double the watercress."

Prosciutto and Gruyere Pinwheels

1 sheet frozen puff pastry, thawed
4 oz thickly sliced prosciutto
2 tbsp chopped fresh basil
1 cup (packed) finely grated Gruyere cheese
1 egg, beaten (for glaze)

1. Place pastry sheet on work surface. Cut in half, forming two rectangles. Arrange half of prosciutto on 1 rectangle, leaving 1-inch border along one side.
2. Sprinkle prosciutto with half of basil, then top with half of cheese. Brush plain border with egg glaze. Starting at long side opposite border, roll up pastry jelly-roll style, pressing gently to seal long edges. Wrap in plastic. Repeat with remaining pastry. Refrigerate until firm, at least 3 hours and up to 2 days.
3. Preheat oven to 400°. Line 2 large baking sheets with parchment paper. Cut logs crosswise into 1-inch-thick rounds. Arrange rounds on prepared sheets. Bake on center rack until pastries are golden, about 16 minutes. Serve warm.

Yield: 30 pieces

Kathleen Glassie

Huitres Vivarois

48 oysters
4 oz white wine
3 tbsp shallots, finely
  chopped
1 tsp garlic, finely chopped
2 tsp curry powder
Juice of one lemon
2 cups fish stock reduced to 4 oz
2 cups heavy cream
1 tsp cornstarch, combined
  with 2 tbsp water
8 oz spinach, cooked
8 oz Gruyere cheese, grated

Preheat oven to 400°.

1. Ask for your oysters to be opened when you buy them. Then place them in a covered baking pan in the refrigerator.
2. In a sauce pan, combine wine, shallots, garlic, curry powder and lemon juice and bring to a boil. Add fish stock and cream, and then add the cornstarch slurry. Bring back to a boil and season with salt and pepper. Let cool.
3. With the oysters (open shell) on a sheet pan, divide and distribute the spinach and then the curry sauce evenly on top of the oysters. Sprinkle with grated cheese and bake for 12 minutes or until the cheese has browned. Serve immediately!

Serves: 8 as an appetizer

From the fabulous Restaurant Bouchard comes this oyster lovers' delight. Chef Bouchard created this dish after a trip to Paris, where he sampled an oyster dish with curry. He wanted more complexity in the dish and added shallots, spinach, and Gruyere cheese, hence the name "Vivarois."

Tuna Tartare

3 3/4 lbs fresh tuna steak or tail
1 1/4 cups olive oil
5 limes, grated zest
1 cup freshly squeezed lime
2 1/2 tsp wasabi powder2
1/2 tbsp soy sauce
2 tbsp Tabasco sauce
2 1/2 tbsp kosher salt
1 1/2 tbsp black pepper
1 1/2 cups minced scallions,
1 sliced jalapeno pepper
5 ripe avocados
1 tbsp sesame seeds

1. Cut the tuna into 1/4-inch dice and place in a large bowl.
2. In a separate bowl, combine the olive oil, lime zest, lime juice, wasabi, soy sauce, Tabasco, salt and pepper. Pour over the tuna. Add the scallions and jalapeno and mix well.
3. Cut the avocados in half, remove the seed and dice to 1/4 inch. Gently fold into the tuna mixture. Add sesame seeds. Allow mixture to sit in the fridge for an hour, letting the flavors mix together. Serve on crackers.

Serves: 40

Shelly Ferrall and Hal Petri
"Our family favorite is Japanese, sesame-flavored rice crackers.
Absolutely the greatest taste for tartare lovers!
Take advantage of the fresh tuna caught right here!"

Roasted Fig and Arugula Salad

1/3 cup wine vinegar or cider vinegar
1 tbsp molasses
2 tsp extra-virgin olive oil
1/4 tsp salt
4 large fresh figs, halved (such as
    Black Mission)
cooking spray
5 cups trimmed arugula
1/4 cup crumbled goat cheese
1/8 tsp freshly ground black pepper

Preheat oven to 425°.

1. Combine first 4 ingredients in a medium bowl, stirring with a whisk. Add figs, toss to coat. Remove figs with a slotted spoon, reserving vinegar mixture.
2. Place figs in a cast-iron or ovenproof skillet coated with cooking spray. Bake for 8 to 10 minutes. Remove the figs from pan; place on a plate. Immediately add reserved vinegar mixture to hot pan, scraping pan to loosen browned bits. Pour into a small bowl; let figs and vinaigrette cool to room temperature.
3. Place arugula on a platter; arrange figs over arugula. Sprinkle with cheese and pepper. Drizzle with cooled vinaigrette.

Serves: 4

Michele Scott

Tucker's Bistro

Warm Heirloom Tomato and Crispy Mozzarella Salad
with Basil Pine Nut Broth

20 cherry mozzarella balls
1/2 cup flour
2 eggs lightly beaten
1 pint Panko, Japanese breadcrumbs
2 quarts oil for frying
1/4 cup washed basil leaves, divided
2 oz pine nuts
3 tbsp water or vegetable stock
4 heirloom tomatoes
French sea salt
fresh ground pepper
extra virgin olive oil

1. Coat mozzarella first in flour, then eggs and finally in breadcrumbs. Set aside.
2. In a large heavy bottomed pot, heat oil to 400°.   Add 1/4 of the basil and fry for 10 seconds; basil may pop in the first few seconds. Set aside. Add mozzarella balls and cook until it starts to brown slightly. Transfer to paper towels and drain.
3. For basil pine nut broth, place 3/4 of the basil, pine nuts and the water or stock in a blender. Puree on high until mixture is smooth. Add salt to taste.
4. To serve, slice each of tomatoes in 4 slices; season lightly with sea salt and pepper. Dress tomatoes with two tablespoons of the basil pine nut broth and divide among four plates.   Place five pieces of mozzarella on each plate with fried basil leaves and finish with olive oil.

Serves: 4

There is nothing like garden fresh tomatoes and basil in the summer and this delicious salad from Tucker's Bistro will have you craving more!

Lobster Fatulli

2- 1 3/4 pound lobsters
2 lbs unsalted butter
1 cup fresh lobster cream or
   prepared lobster bisque
1 cup potato gnocchi
6 - 8 small button mushrooms
2 tsp white vinegar
1/4 lb salt pork
1 cup chopped tomatoes
1/2 cup grated Parmesan cheese
20 leaves flat leaf parsley
salt and white pepper to taste
fresh chervil or chives for garnish

1. Bring 3 gallons of water to a boil. Cook lobster for 9 minutes or until tender. Set aside two teaspoons of butter and melt remaining butter. Remove lobster meat from its shell and add to melted butter. Reserve in a saucepan over low heat.

2. In a shallow sauté pan, add lobster cream (lobster stock & heavy cream or lobster bisque) and potato gnocchi. Cook over medium heat until tender.

3. In a small saucepan, add 4 cups of water and vinegar to blanch the button mushrooms. Strain the mushrooms.

4. Soak the salt pork in water for 5-10 minutes to bleed out any extra salt. Trim the skin off and reserve the white pork fat. In a small sauté pan at medium heat, render the salt pork until golden brown. Drain off excess fat.

5. In the same pan as the gnocchi, add the button mushrooms, chopped tomatoes, and salt pork. Simmer for 1 minute and then finish with Parmesan cheese, parsley, 2 teaspoons butter, salt and pepper.

6. To serve, spoon the gnocchi and mushrooms into a pasta bowl and then arrange the lobster meat on top. Garnish with fresh chervil or chives.

Serves: 2

The Lobster Fatulli dish is an original concept of Executive Chef Rob Biela. This dish is named after Newport business legend Ron Fatulli, owner of the Aquidneck Lobster Company.

A *Newport Summer Moment...*

*"One of my favorite Newport summer moments is
taking a walk on the beach on a warm summer evening at sunset. The air smells sweet
and fresh, the sky is blazing red and purple, the ocean ripples softly onto the beach, and
there is a gentle breeze to keep the mosquitos at bay...
That's a glorious Newport moment!"*

—Leslie Holloway

Tenderloin Stuffed with Lobster

Tenderloin:
2 4-lb beef tenderloins, trimmed
salt & pepper to taste
16-20 oz lobster tail meat
1 1/2 tsp lemon juice
1 tbsp butter

Bearnaise Sauce:
1/2 cup red wine vinegar
1/2 cup dry white wine
4 shallots or green onions, finely
   chopped
8 whole black peppercorns, crushed
8 egg yolks
1 cup clarified butter
1/2 tsp tarragon
dash of salt
dash lemon juice

Preheat oven to 350°.

1. Trim off tips of tenderloins to make 11-inch cylinders; rub tenderloin with dry paper towel. In a large skillet, sear tenderloins one at a time, on all sides. Butterfly each tenderloin lengthwise by cutting the roast to within 1/2 inch of the bottom. Lay tenderloins open. Pat meat firmly until about 1/2 inch thick. Season with salt and pepper.

2. Arrange the lobster pieces atop each tenderloin along one lengthwise edge, in a row. Drizzle lemon juice and butter over lobster. Close the tenderloin meat around the lobster. Roll the meat firmly keeping the lobster pieces centered inside. Secure meat rolls with kitchen string, tying at 1-inch intervals.

3. Bake for 45-55 minutes on middle rack (135° - 140° internal temperature).

4. Bearnaise Sauce: Combine wine vinegar, wine, shallots, and crushed peppercorn in a heavy saucepan and boil over medium heat until only 2 tablespoons of liquid remain. Remove pan from heat and whisk in the egg yolks.

5. Pour mixture into double boiler, whisking until the yolks turn pale yellow and sauce thickens to the consistency of mayonnaise. Little by little, whisk in the clarified butter, then the crushed tarragon, salt and lemon juice. Sauce can be kept warm over a pan of hot water, not boiling.

6. To serve, remove strings from tenderloin. Let stand 10 minutes before carving. Slice and serve with Bearnaise sauce. Serve sauce warm, but not piping hot.
   Serves: 16

Tamara Farrick

"This is a very expensive dish, but very impressive. If you are too nervous to butterfly the tenderloin yourself, ask the butcher. I find that an electric knife works well. The meat is quite simple to prepare and can be put together a day in advance. The Bearnaise Sauce can be fickle; if you have never made it, you may want to take a practice run. Some sauce tips: Have all ingredients at room temperature, butter should be warm, even hot, but not bubbling. If the sauce curdles, try whisking it, little by little into a bowl with 1 tablespoon cold water."

Mid-Summer Night's Salad

Fish:
1/2 bottle dark rum
1 10-oz bottle peach nectar
6 8-ounce striped bass fillets, skin on
2 tbsp finely chopped fresh summer
   herbs: basil, sage, chives, lavender
2 cloves garlic, minced
1 tbsp ground black pepper
coarse salt, to taste

Salad:
1 lb organic, young field lettuce
3 heirloom tomatoes
12 fingerling potatoes
1/2 lb macadamia nuts, toasted

Piperade:
4 tbsp finely chopped fresh summer
   herbs: basil, sage, chives,
   lavender
5 cloves garlic, minced
1/4 cup white balsamic vinegar
1/2 cup extra virgin olive oil
1 tbsp Dijon mustard
1 red bell pepper
1 green pepper
1 yellow pepper
2 jalapeno peppers
1 large ripe tomato
1 small onion, peeled and cut into
   1/4-inch rounds
lemon juice
salt and pepper to taste

1. Fish: In a sauce pan, bring the rum to a simmer and add the peach nectar. Reduce until syrupy and let cool to room temperature. Score the skin (cut barely through the skin) on the bass fillets. Marinate in the herbs, garlic, salt and pepper.

2. Salad: Wash the field lettuce. Cut the tomatoes into 1/4-inch thick half moons. Place potatoes in a pan, cover with cold, salted water and bring to a simmer. Cook until tender, drain and let cool. Once cool, cut the potatoes in half lengthwise.

3. Piperade: Mix the herbs, garlic, vinegar and olive oil together with Dijon mustard. Mix until smooth and emulsified. In separate containers, marinate the peppers, tomatoes and onions with the dressing. Grill the peppers until the skin blisters thoroughly. Grill the tomatoes and onions, let cool. Save the excess marinade from each. Peel, seed and rough chop the peppers, cutting the jalapeño very fine. Roughly chop the onions and tomatoes. Combine everything together and mix with leftover marinade. Season with lemon juice, salt and pepper.

Finish:
Preheat the grill, very, very hot!

4. Grill the fish, flesh side down first. Grill until nicely marked, turn onto the skin side and baste periodically with rum-peach syrup. Grill until the fish is just cooked through, with no translucent flesh.

5. Toss the lettuce with potatoes, nuts and piperade. Divide the salad and potato evenly between six plates or bowls. Arrange the heirloom slices on top and place the fish on salad directly from the grill. Serve immediately with grilled or toasted Tuscan style bread.

Serves: 6 as an entreé

This incredible recipe from Chef Casey Riley is truly a "must-try" for anyone.
It is a great one for the outdoor grill and if you really want to show off,
let your friends know the recipe has been featured on the Food Network.

Pan Seared Scallops with Orange Mascarpone Sauce,
Tomato Ceviche and Toasted Orzo "Mac and Cheese"

Orange mascarpone sauce:
2 cups orange juice
1 cups heavy cream
1/2 cup salted butter
1/2 cup mascarpone cheese

Cherry tomato ceviche:
1 pint each red cherry tomatoes and
  yellow teardrop tomatoes, cut in
  quarters
1 red pepper, diced
1 seedless cucumber
1 poblano pepper, diced, seeded
1/2 cup orange juice
1/4 cup each lemon and lime juice
3 tbsp ketchup
2 tbsp chives, chopped
2 tbsp cilantro, chopped
1 small bunch scallions

Mac and Cheese:
4 cups orzo pasta
1 tbsp olive oil
2 cloves garlic, chopped
1 shallot, chopped
1 cup heavy cream
3 tbsp salted butter
1/2 cup Asiago cheese, shredded
basil, finely chopped in strips

4 tbsp canola oil
20 fresh native sea scallops

Preheat oven to 350°.

Orange Mascarpone Sauce: In a medium saucepan, at medium heat, reduce the orange juice by half and then add the heavy cream. Reduce until mixture is thick. Once thick, stir in the butter and mascarpone cheese. Stir constantly as the sauce has a tendency to break when not whipped.

Cherry Tomato Ceviche: Combine all ingredients and reserve.

Toasted orzo Mac and Cheese:

1. Place orzo on a baking sheet and place in oven for ten minutes, or until golden brown. Once pasta is golden brown, cook in boiling salted water until al dente in texture. (Al dente means there should be a slight resistance in the center when the pasta is chewed.)

2. Once cooked, pour the pasta into a colander and spread ice over the pasta, to "shock it" and stop the cooking process. Reserve.

3. In a sauté pan, heat olive oil, and add garlic and shallot. Cook at medium heat for five minutes until soft.

4. Add heavy cream and pasta to sauté pan, until thoroughly mixed. Add butter, basil chiffonade and Asiago cheese. Reserve.

Finish:

In a sauté pan at medium high heat, place four tablespoons canola oil and heat. Add scallops and sear, 3 -4 minutes per side, cooking until just translucent. Place scallops in the center of serving plate with orzo mac and cheese surrounding them. Top scallops with orange sauce and a spoonful of tomato ceviche.

Serves: 4

The famously fantastic A&O Restaurant Group, owners of Asterisk, A O Fish and The Boulangerie have shared this recipe, a self described "party in your mouth!"

Seared Local Striped Bass

with Apricot Quinoa and Mushroom Fennel Vinaigrette

1 cup quinoa
1/2 cup water
1/2 cup white wine
1 sprig tarragon
1/2 cup dried apricots
juice from 1 lemon
4 oz. extra virgin olive oil, divided
4 oz shiitake or oyster mushrooms
    stems picked and reserved
2 fennel bulbs thinly sliced
2 tbsp sherry vinegar
salt and pepper to taste
4 6-oz fillets of bass

Preheat oven to 400°.

1. Cook quinoa according to package instructions, set aside.

2. Combine water, white wine and 5 tarragon leaves in a 2 quart sauce pot. Bring to boil, add dried apricots, turn heat off. Cover pot and let steep for 20 minutes. Strain out apricots and reserve cooking liquid.

3. When cool, thinly slice apricots and add to quinoa. Season quinoa salad with 1 tablespoon lemon juice, 2 tablespoons olive oil and remaining tarragon leaves.

4. Return liquid to stove and reduce down with mushroom stems, few slices of fennel and 1 teaspoon sherry vinegar. Reduce until 1 oz. liquid remains. Strain liquid into a small container and season with salt, pepper and top with 1 table-spoon olive oil.

5. Prepare vinaigrette by heating a sauté pan over a high flame. When pan is hot add 2 tablespoons olive oil and fennel. Gently sauté for 2 minutes. Add mush-rooms and continue cooking for 10 minutes more, stirring occasionally. Season with salt and a splash of sherry vinegar.

6. Heat Teflon pan over a high flame, add 1 tablespoon olive oil to pan. Season fish with salt and pepper and sear until golden brown. Flip and roast in oven for 5 minutes. When fish is easily pierced with the tip of a knife, the fish is done. Remove from oven and set aside.

7. To plate: Divide quinoa among the four plates, place bass on top, spoon mush-room and fennel over the fish and drizzle the vinaigrette around.

Serves: 4

If a romantic dinner with exquisite food and atmosphere is what you are looking for, Tucker's Bistro is the place to be. Tucker's keeps the menu seasonal and fresh, just like this fantastic local striped bass recipe.

A Bellevue Dinner

5TH GRADE, CLASS OF 2009

Sea Salt Crusted Tuna with Shallot Cream Sauce

Tuna:
1 oz sea salt
4 oz Panko (Japanese breadcrumbs)
2 sprigs fresh thyme
2 leaves fresh basil
8 oz tuna loin
2 oz canola oil

Shallot cream sauce:
2 oz shallots
1/2 cup white wine
1/2 cup heavy cream
4 oz butter

1. Place salt, Panko, thyme and basil in a food processor and ground to a fine consistency. Cut tuna loin in half and coat with bread crumb mixture. Set aside.
2. Prepare shallot cream sauce by finely chopping shallots and place into small pan. Add white wine and reduce by half. Add cream and reduce by half. Turn off heat and mix in butter until butter is completely melted.
3. Sear tuna loin in a sauté pan with canola oil unitl golden brown on all sides.
4. Serve tuna with shallot cream sauce and is best accompanied by roasted potatoes and sautéed greens.

Serves: 2

This elegant tuna dish with delicate flavoring will have your guests thinking you slaved for hours. Thank you to Pronto owner and Executive Chef James Cavanaugh for keeping it simple!

Grilled Asparagus with Balsamic Vinegar

1 lb thin asparagus spears
1 tsp olive oil
1/4 tsp kosher salt
1/8 tsp freshly ground black
   pepper
cooking spray
1 tbsp balsamic vinegar

Prepare grill.
1. Snap off ends of asparagus; place in bowl or shallow dish. Drizzle asparagus with oil; sprinkle with salt and pepper, tossing well to coat.
2. Place asparagus on a grill rack coated with cooking spray; grill 2 minutes on each side or until crisp-tender.
3. Place asparagus in a bowl, drizzle with vinegar. Serve immediately.

Serves: 4

Ginger Algiere

A Newport Summer Moment...
"The simplicity and beauty of the ever changing sunsets over Narragansett Bay is what gives the palette of Newport its unique beauty!"

-Diane Canepari

Tricolor Potatoes with Pesto and Parmesan

8 tbsp olive oil
1 cup (packed) fresh basil leaves
2 large shallots
4 garlic cloves
salt and pepper
cooking spray
1 1/2 lbs red-skinned new potatoes
1 1/2 lbs Yukon Gold potatoes
   (each about 1 1/2 inches round)
1 lb purple potatoes (each about
   1 1/2 inches round)
1/2 cup freshly grated Parmesan
   cheese

Preheat oven to 400°.

1. Blend 4 tablespoons olive oil, basil, shallots, and garlic in processor until smooth. Season basil sauce with salt and pepper to taste.
2. In a large bowl, toss all potatoes with 4 tablespoons olive oil, salt, and pepper to coat. Transfer potatoes to a large baking sheet prepared with cooking spray.
3. Roast potatoes until almost tender, about 35 minutes.
4. Pour basil sauce over potatoes and toss to coat. Continue roasting potatoes until golden brown and tender when pierced with skewer, about 20 minutes longer. Transfer potatoes to serving bowl. Add cheese and toss to coat.

Serves: 10

Monique Burgess

"Basil sauce can be made 8 hours ahead and refrigerated."

Grilled Artichokes with Olive Oil, Lemon and Mint

2 lemons, halved
6 large artichokes
2/3 cup extra-virgin olive oil
1/3 cup fresh lemon juice
3 tbsp chopped fresh mint
salt and pepper

1. Squeeze juice from halved lemons into large bowl filled with cold water. Cut stems off artichokes, leaving about 1 inch. Snap off outer 2 rows of leaves. Cut off top 1/3 of artichoke. Quarter artichoke lengthwise. Using small knife, cut out choke and prickly small leaves. Place artichokes in lemon water.
2. Bring large pot of salted water to boil. Drain artichokes, add to pot, and boil until crisp-tender, about 15 minutes. Drain and transfer artichokes to rack and cool.
3. Prepare grill (medium-high heat).
4. Whisk oil, lemon juice, and mint in small bowl. Season dressing to taste with salt and pepper.
5. Brush artichokes with dressing. Grill until tender and lightly charred in spots, turning occasionally, about 8 minutes. Transfer artichokes to platter. Drizzle with some of remaining dressing. Serve warm or at room temperature.

Serves: 6

Bethany Di Napoli

Wild Mushroom Risotto

5 cups low-sodium chicken broth
1 1/2 cups water
1 tbsp olive oil
1/2 stick unsalted butter
1/4 lb fresh wild mushrooms such
   as porcini, trimmed and chopped
1/3 cup finely chopped shallots
1 1/2 cups Arborio rice
1/2 to 1 tsp white truffle oil
   (optional)
1 1/2 oz finely grated Parmigiano
   Reggiano (3/4 cup)
1 tsp chopped fresh chives
salt and pepper

1. Bring chicken broth and water to a simmer in a 4-quart pot and keep at a bare simmer, covered.
2. Heat oil with 1 tablespoon butter in a 4- to 5-quart heavy saucepan over moderately high heat, then sauté mushrooms, stirring occasionally, until browned and any liquid they give off is evaporated, about 4 minutes. Season with salt and pepper, then transfer to a bowl.
3. Cook shallots in 2 tablespoons butter in same saucepan over moderate heat, stirring, until softened, about 3 minutes. Add rice and cook, stirring, 1 minute.
4. Ladle in 1 cup simmering stock and cook at a strong simmer, stirring, until absorbed. Continue simmering and adding stock, about 1/2 cup at a time, stirring very frequently and letting each addition be absorbed before adding next, until rice is just tender and creamy-looking, 16 to 18 minutes. (Save leftover stock for thinning.)
5. Remove from heat and stir in remaining tablespoon butter, sautéed mushrooms, truffle oil to taste (if using), cheese, chives, and salt and pepper to taste. If desired, thin risotto with some of leftover stock.

Serves: 4

Carole Di Napoli

Lemon Granita

2 1/4 cups water
1/2 cup confectionary sugar
1 cup lemon juice (4-5 lemons)
finely grated zest of 1 lemon

1. In a heavy non-reactive pan, boil water and sugar. Cook until reduced by almost half. Remove from heat and cool.
2. Add lemon juice and zest. Pour into shallow trays and freeze for 20-30 minutes.
3. Use a fork to break up ice crystals and repeat process of freezing and breaking up a few more times. Or use gelato or ice cream maker. Serve immediately.

Serves: 4-6

Jeff Hodges

"Based on a recipe from the Café Cookbook."

Chocolate Decadence

4 oz quality bittersweet chocolate
   (not unsweetened)
1 stick unsalted butter
3/4 cup sugar
3 large eggs
1/2 cup unsweetened cocoa powder,
   plus additional for sprinkling
vanilla sorbet, if desired

Preheat oven to 375°.

1. Butter an 8-inch round cake pan. Line bottom with a round of wax paper and butter paper.

2. Chop chocolate into small pieces. In a double boiler set over a saucepan of barely simmering water, melt chocolate with unsalted butter, stirring until smooth. Remove top of double boiler from heat and whisk sugar into chocolate mixture. Add eggs and whisk well.

3. Sift cocoa powder over chocolate mixture and whisk until just combined. Pour batter into pan and bake on middle rack for 25 minutes, or until top has formed a thin crust. Cool cake in pan on a rack 5 minutes and invert onto a serving plate.

4. Dust cake with additional cocoa powder and serve with sorbet, if desired.

Serves: 6

Diane Canepari

Vanilla Roasted Strawberries

2 tbsp unsalted butter
1 vanilla bean, split lengthwise
24 fresh strawberries, tops removed
2 tbsp light brown sugar
3 tbsp dry red wine
1 1/2 tbsp balsamic vinegar
1 tbsp chilled unsalted butter, cut
   into small pieces

Preheat oven to 400°.

1. Melt 2 tablespoons butter in a 9-inch baking pan in oven. Scrape seeds from vanilla bean into melted butter; combine.

2. Place strawberries, cut side down, in pan; sprinkle with sugar.

3. Tuck vanilla halves between berries in bottom of pan. Bake for 10 minutes or until berries are soft. Cool for 20 minutes.

4. Remove berries from pan, and transfer pan juices to a small skillet. Add wine and vinegar to pan; bring to a simmer over medium heat. Remove from heat; whisk in chilled butter.

5. Drizzle sauce over berries. Serve immediately.

Serves: 4

Krista Peterson

Cliff Walk To-Go

Cliff Walk

The Cliff Walk of Newport is world famous as a public access walk and remains one of Newport's most popular tourist attractions. Beginning at Easton's Beach on Memorial Blvd. and ending at Bailey's Beach on the south end of Bellevue Ave., this spectacular 3.5-mile walk combines the natural beauty of the Newport shoreline with the architectural history of Newport's Gilded Age. Most of the walk is in easy walking condition and is enjoyed by people of all ages. So put on your walking shoes and hit this breathtaking trail; you will never tire of the panoramic vistas and architectural wonders along the way.

About the Artist

Joan Boghossian, "Cliff Walk II"

Joan Boghossian, a graduate of the University of Rhode Island, studied art locally and nationally. She has won more than sixty significant prizes, including awards in national and regional juried shows. She is a four- time winner of the Grumbacher Gold Medallion Award in watercolor. Her awards cover watercolors, oil, etchings, and monotypes.

Joan is an elected artist member of numerous art associations, including the New England Watercolor Society, the Providence Art Club, the Copley Society of Boston, the Catherine Lorillard Wolfe Art Club, and the Mystic Art Association. A native of Newport, Joan lives in Pawtucket and maintains a studio in Narragansett and Providence. Her paintings can be found in Newport at Spring Bull Gallery.

Cliff Walk To-Go

On those gorgeous summer days when you stay at the beach a little later than you planned, or decide to go for an afternoon sail because the winds are perfect, you just may not have the time to prepare your next meal. So we decided to make it easy for you and help you find some of Newport's best food "to-go."

Whether it is breakfast, lunch or dinner you need, or just a snack, you will find a place to get it here in our Cliff Walk To-Go section. We chose some of our favorite places to get take-out and then asked for their most popular take-out items; they are listed here. We are sure you will find something to tickle your tastebuds at any of these great places! Have fun!

Anthony's Seafood
963 Aquidneck Avenue, Middletown
401-846-9620
If it is seafood you want, Anthony's is the place. Both a seafood market and restaurant, you can find fresh fish, ready-to-cook appetizers and entreés and, of course, a full menu of seafood take-out!

Fish & Chips   Fisherman's Platter   All Chowders

Aquidneck Restaurant & Pizzeria
27 Aquidneck Avenue, Middletown
401-849-3356
www.AQPizza.com
If you've just spent the day at Easton's Beach, stop here; it's right across the street. You can pick-up your dinner to-go!

Chicken Florentine Pizza   Aquidneck Pasta with Feta and Chicken   AQ Specialty Baked Stuffed Eggplant

Boulangerie
382 Spring Street, Newport
401-846-3377
The best croissants in Newport are here! Not to mention ready-to-go sandwiches on crusty bread and fabulous desserts! This quaint little European café will capture your heart!

Almond Croissant   Fruit Tarts   Chocolate Croissants

The Market Newport Gourmet
43 Memorial Boulevard, Newport
401-848-2600
www.newportgourmet.com
All your to-go needs can be met here: sandwiches to order, blue plate dinner specials, gourmet prepared foods, fresh produce, and a fantastic bakery...what else could you ask for!

Mr. Price's Chicken Salad   N.E. Clam Chowder   Chicken Pot Pie

A Newport Summer Moment...

"One of our favorite Newport summer moments is walking the Cliff Walk from Narragansett Ave. to First Beach, dipping our toes in the water and picking up some nice ice-cold Del's from the truck in the parking lot.

Another favorite moment of ours is flying kites down on the tip of the island. The wind is always blowing, there are always lots of kites flying, and it is great to lay back on the grass and watch them dipping and swirling overhead."

-Jess and Todd Working

Cliff Walk

GRADE 3, CLASS OF 2011

Max's Market

471 Thames Street, Newport
401-849-8088
www.maxsmarket.com

Before boarding your boat for a sail, stop in here to pick up great gourmet sandwiches, the finest selection of cheeses and unique specialty foods! If it's provisioning you need, they can do it for you!

Curried Chicken Salad Sandwich   Thai Chicken Cakes
Tomato, Mozzarella & Salami Bagel Sandwich

Portabella

136 Broadway, Newport
401-847-8200

Homemade Italian breads daily, prepared Italian dishes, hot and cold Italian sandwiches...Now that's Italian!!

Alla Rahmani Sandwich with Eggplant, Artichokes & Hot
Peppers   Tomato Basil Soup   Foccaccia

Roba Dolce

448 Thames Street, Newport
401-272-0777
www.robadolce.com

If you are taking an evening stroll on lower Thames, definitely stop in for some gelato. The open-air café and music will make you think you are in Italy!

Italian Chicken Panini   Pints of Gelato   Biscotti

Sig's Deli

7 Carroll Avenue, Newport
401-847-9668

On your way out for a ride around Ocean Drive? Stop at Sig's to pick up your picnic luch or dinner; a real local landmark!

Sig's Macaroni and Cheese   Fresh Breast of Chicken Salad
Sandwich   Roasted Turkey with Cranberry Sauce Sandwich &
Dinner To-Go

Thai Cuisine

517 Thames Street, Newport
401-841-8822

It wasn't that many years ago that we couldn't get Thai food in Newport. Hard to believe, we know. Thank you Thai Cuisine for finally stepping up to the plate, and serving us our favorite Thai dishes!

Thailand Madness   Mango Curry   Hunan Duck

Tito's Cantina

651 West Main Road, Middletown
401-849-4222
www.titos.com

Tito's has the best authentic Mexican food on the island. When you want to add a little spice to life, stop by Tito's!

Macho Nachos   Tito's Enchilada Trio   Southwestern Chicken
Chimichanga

A Newport Summer Moment...

"What I love best about Newport in the summer is.... the smell of the Rosa Rugosa roses that bloom in June and July mixed with the salty sea air as I walk with my family along Cliff Walk.
What a wonderful sensory pleasure!
One year my kids and I walked the Cliff Walk in four parts (four different days)
and made maps of all the great things we saw or found along the way—mansions, flowers, tunnels, seals!
My son was able to put all the hand-drawn maps together and remember all the parts along the way."

-Lisa Pritchard

Traditional Newport Clambake for 20

When we think of summers in Newport, the shore, fresh seafood, and families and friends getting together, the idea of a traditional clambake on the beach seems to fit right in. So we decided to include a section in our cookbook, for those ambitious, clambake enthusiasts, on how to have an authentic clambake.

For the how-to's, we went right to the local experts, McGrath's Clambakes, Inc., and asked them to share their secrets with us. Of course, should you decide you just want to kick back and let someone else do all the work for you, McGrath's will happily accommodate you, wherever you are!

Ingredients:

- 20 1 1/4 or 1 1/2 lb. lobsters, rubber bands removed
- 10 lbs steamers (soft-shelled clams), washed
- 10 lbs mussels, washed and debearded
- 20 ears sweet corn, outer layers of husk peeled, stalk and silk ends trimmed
- 40 red bliss potatoes, washed
- 20 yellow onions, peeled
- 5 lbs Chorico links (spicy Portuguese sausage), cut in 1- inch pieces
- 5 lbs cod fish, divided into 4 oz. portions wrapped in small brown paper lunch bags
- 5 lbs melted butter

For Food Preparation:

Portion food equally into 20 cheese cloth bags (one per guest). Layout large piece of cheese-cloth and stack food in center (vegetables on the bottom and shellfish dispersed on top). Draw corners of cheese cloth together loosely and tie into a "bag."

Special Requirements:

- Cheesecloth
- 5 Bushels of Seaweed (must be Rockweed with air bubbles)
- Approximately 20 to 25, 8- to 10-inch diameter rocks (granite field stone works best)
- 6 old shipping pallets (old oak pallets work best — be sure pallets are clean of any paint, etc.), or a comparable amount of driftwood from a beach. Do not use cord wood, it will burn too slow.
- 6 to 8 Heavy Gauge Canvas Tarps. Tarps must be clean and untreated with any type of water repellant chemicals (in the absence of canvas tarps, additional seaweed can be put over the food and then covered with several layers of burlap, topped with more seaweed to cover and weigh down the burlap)
- 1 Pitchfork, for tending fire
- 1 Gravel Rake, for tending fire
- 1 Garden Hose, to wet canvas

For Clambake Fire:

1.) Always check with local fire officials to obtain necessary burn permits.

2.) If clambake is on a beach, clear loose sand until you reach a firm base for your clambake. It is not necessary to dig a deep hole. For dirt or grassy surfaces, it is not necessary to dig a hole, however, the base area should be flat and it should be noted that grass will be burned.

3.) Make a stack of 4 pallets and then cover the 4th pallet with the rocks. Stack remaining 2 pallets on top of the rocks.

4.) The fire should be lit using crumpled newspaper at the base of the stack of pallets.

5.) With the use of pallets, the clambake fire will burn very hot and very fast for the first 1/2 hour. For safety purposes, the fire should never be left unattended.

6.) The fire will take about an hour to burn off and settle down to a bed of coals and hot rocks. At this point, any remaining pieces of wood should be raked out of the fire in preparation to put the clambake on.

7.) Completely wet canvas with hose.

To Put on Clambake:

1.) The Clambake process should be done quickly but carefully, to capture as much heat and steam as possible.

2.) Spread seaweed over the hot rock base. The seaweed should be layered thicker in the center of the clambake; however, take care that there are no exposed rocks on the sides of the clambake as well.

3.) Layer the 20 bags of food on the seaweed starting in the center.

4.) Cover the food with the 6 to 8 layers of canvas that have been previously wet.

5.) During the first hour of cooking, dampen the canvas with the garden hose periodically (approximately every 10 to 15 minutes)

6.) During the second hour of cooking the canvas may need to be dampened only several times.

7.) After two hours, gather guests around and slowly peel away the layers of canvas as to maximize the suspense. A billowing cloud of steam will rise and reveal a bed of brightly colored food.

8.) Serve one bag of food per guest; accompany with drawn butter.

McGrath Clambakes, Inc.
64 Halsey Street #5, Newport, RI 02840
Phone: 401-847-7743   Fax: 401-847-0340

www.riclambake.com ~ E-mail: info@riclambake.com

Clam Chowder

Roux:
1/2 cup salted butter
3 cups onions, diced
1 cup flour

Stock:
1 quart minced sea clams
1 1/2 quarts natural clam juice
1 1/2 quarts half & half
1 pound potatoes, peeled and diced
dash Spanish paprika

Prepare Roux: Melt butter in heay stockpot. Add and sauté onions until clear. Add the flour and blend; cook 2-4 minutes over low heat, stiring frequentlly. Set aside to cool.

Prepare Stock: In a separate pot, bring to boil clams and natural clam juice. Let simmer for 15-20 minutes. In another pot, peel and dice potatoes; cook until soft in boiling water. Drain and set aside.

Final Preparation:
1. Add hot stock to cooled roux and whisk. Whisk thouroughly until smooth. Slowly bring to a boil.
2. Reduce heat and add coooked potatoes.
3. Carefully whisk in half & half (do not smash potatoes). The amount of half and half depends on desired taste. Simmer 5-10 minutes.
4. Serve in warm soup bowls. Sprinkle with a dash of Spanish paprika. Enjoy!
    Serves: 8

No clambake is complete without a delicious bowl of clam chowder to start things off. Enjoy this recipe at your clambake or just stop down at The Mooring Restaurant and enjoy it out on their deck while admiring the spectacular sunsets and bustling harbor!

A Newport Summer Moment...

"The one thing I love about summer in Newport is being able to go out on our boat and raft up with friends, swim in the cove with the kids and enjoy a meal of fresh seafood."
-Whitey Russell

St. Michael's Country Day School

Located near the heart of downtown Newport, Rhode Island, St. Michael's Country Day School is an independent, coeducational, nondenominational school for children from Preschool through eighth grade. The school sits on a spacious seven-acre campus, with distant views of the Atlantic Ocean. The California Mission style main building, with its distinct red tile roof, was built in 1898 as a summer home for sisters Ellen and Ida Mason from Boston.

Today, St. Michael's Country Day School is a vibrant school with strong leadership, committed, dynamic teachers; a challenging curriculum that sets it apart. Equally as important in the culture of the school is teaching respect for others, and respect for one's self. Founded in 1938, it is the mission of the school "to educate the whole child: mind, body, spirit, and character." The arts at St. Michael's — including the visual and computer arts, active and engaging drama and music programs — are wholly integrated into the daily life of the school and its curriculum. Class sizes are small; with an average of twelve to fourteen students.

The St. Michael's Parents Association is one of the major fundraisers for the school. It is the goal of the PA to enhance the quality of life on the school's campus, and to support the teachers in their efforts. Field trips and assemblies, computers and computer equipment, art supplies and theater equipment, are all made possible by money raised throughout the school year by the PA, on projects such as this cookbook, Flavors of a Newport Summer.

Contributing Restaurants and Inns

We gratefully acknowledge the following restaurants and inns for generously contributing to our cookbook. We hope you visit them and enjoy their great food and hospitality!

22 Bowen's Wine Bar and Grille, p.61
22 Bowen's Wharf, Newport
401-841-8884
www.22bowens.com

Asterisk, p.21, 98
599 Thames Street, Newport
401-841-8833

The Atlantic Beach Club, p.64
55 Purgatory Road, Middletown
401-847-2750
www.atlanticbeachclub.com

The Black Pearl, p.37
Bannister's Wharf, Newport
401-846-5264
www.blackpearlnewport.com

Brick Alley Pub & Restaurant, p.56
140 Thames Street, Newport
401-849-6334
www.brickalley.com

Café Zelda, p.62, 71
528 Thames Street, Newport
401-849-4002
www.cafezelda.com

Castle Hill Inn & Resort, p.97
590 Ocean Drive, Newport
401-849-3800
www.castlehillinn.com

Cheeky Monkey Café, p.15
14 Perry Mill Wharf, Newport
401-845-9494
www.cheekymonkeycafe.com

Clarke Cooke House, p.56
Bannister's Wharf, Newport
401-849-2900
www.clarkecooke.com

La Farge Perry House, p.88
24 Kay Street, Newport
401-847-2223
www.lafargeperry.com

Le Bistro, p.50
41 Bowen's Wharf, Newport
401-849-7778
www.lebistronewport.com

The Mooring Restaurant, p.112
Sayers Wharf, Newport
401-846-2260
www.mooringrestaurant.com

Norey's, p.32
156 Broadway, Newport
401-847-4971

Pronto Restaurant, p.57, 101
464 Thames Street, Newport
401-847-5251
www.prontonewport.com

Restaurant Bouchard, p.93
505 Thames Street, Newport
401-846-0123
www.restaurantbouchard.com

Sakonnet Fish Company, p.33
657 Park Avenue, Portsmouth
401-683-1180
www.sakonnetfish.com

Samuel Durfee House, p.23
352 Spring St, Newport
401-847-1652 or 877-696-2374
www.samueldurfeehouse.com

The Spiced Pear Restaurant, p.32, 58
117 Memorial Boulevard, Newport
401-847-2244
www.spicedpear.com

Tucker's Bistro, p.94, 99
150 Broadway, Newport
401-846-3449
www.tuckersbistro.com

The West Deck, p.95
One Waite's Wharf, Newport
401-847-3610
www.westdeck.com

Yesterday's, p.82
28 Washington Square, Newport
401-847-0125
www.yesterdaysandtheplace.com

Our hat's off to you!

Focused on *your success!*

banknewport.com
800.234.8586

Artists and Galleries

We are very fortunate to have so many talented artists living in Newport and we are proud to present some of their work here in our book. We are grateful and appreciative to those artists and galleries who have collaborated with us on this book and encourage you to take the time to discover more about them by visiting the galleries listed below!

Artists

James Allen
www.jamesallenart.com

Diane Gay
Spring Bull Gallery

Brian Becken
Roger King Fine Arts

Peter Hussey
The Harrison Gallery

Joan Boghossian
Spring Bull Gallery

Paola Mangiacapra
Spring Bull Gallery

Ray Caram
Spring Bull Gallery

Kate Hoyt Psaki
Arnold Art
and
Newport Fine Arts

Victoria Corey
Arnold Art
and
Jamestown Designs

Eveline Roberge
Fisher Gallery

Galleries

Arnold Art
210 Thames Street
Newport, RI 02840
(401) 847-2273 or
1-800-352-2234
www.arnoldart.com

Jamestown Designs
17 Narragansett Avenue
Jamestown, RI 02835
(401) 423-0344
www.jamestowndesigns.com

Fisher Gallery
136 Bellevue Avenue
Newport, RI 02840
(401) 849-7446

Newport Fine Arts
135 Spring Street
Newport, RI 02840
(401) 848-0358

Five Main Gallery
5 Main Street
Wickford, RI 02852
(401) 294-6280

Roger King Fine Arts
21 Bowen's Wharf
Newport, RI 02840
(401) 847-4359
www.rkingfinearts.com

The Harrison Gallery
39 Spring Street
Williamstown, MA 01267
(413) 458-1700
www.theharrisongallery.com

Spring Bull Gallery
55 Bellevue Avenue
Newport, RI 02840
(401) 849-9166
www.springbullgallery.com

INTERIORS

Curtains Furniture Upholstery Fabrics Carpet Slipcovers

ANTIQUES & DECORATIONS

John Peixinho
121 Bellevue Avenue
Newport, Rhode Island 02840
Tel. 401-847-8311

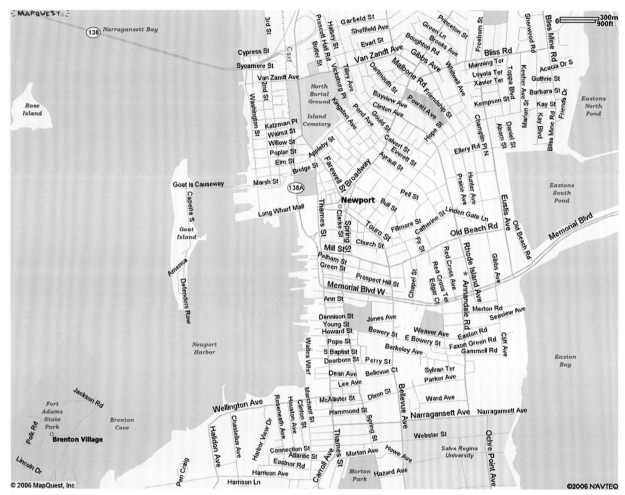

MAPQUEST

138 Narragansett Bay

Rose Island

Goat Is Causeway

Goat Island

Capella S

America

Defenders Row

Newport Harbor

Fort Adams State Park

Jackson Rd

Polk Rd

Brenton Village

Lincoln Dr

Brenton Cove

3rd St

Cypress St
Sycamore St

Van Zandt Ave

C St

Washington St
Van 2nd St

Katzman Pl
Walnut St
Willow St
Poplar St
Elm St

Marsh St

Long Wharf Mall

North Burial Ground

Island Cemetery

Prescott Hall Rd
Butler St

Halsey St
Tilley Ave
Vicksburg St

Garfield St
Sheffield Ave
Evart St

Van Zandt Ave
Dartmouth St
Bayview Ave
Clinton Ave

Kingston Ave
Pond Ave
Gould St

Appleby St

Farewell St

Broadway

Newport

Thames St

Spring St
Clarke St

Bridge St

Touro St

Church St

Mill St

Pelham St
Green St

Prospect Hill St

Memorial Blvd W

Ann St

Chapel St

Green Ln
Brooks Ave
Boughton Rd
Gibbs Ave
Malbone Rd
Powell Ave
Friendship St
Hope St

Calvert St
Everett St
Ayrault St

Pell St

Bull St

Fillmore St

Fir St

Princeton St
Whitwell Ave

Freeborn St

Bliss Rd

Manning Ter
Loyola Ter
Xavier Ter

Kempsen St

Champlin St

Ellery Rd

Hunter Ave
Prairie Ave

Linden Gate Ln

Catherine St

Red Cross St
Red Cross Ter
Edgar Ct

Rhode Island Ave

Old Beach Rd

Annandale Rd

Sherwood Rd
Keeher Ave
Toppa Blvd

Marion St

Daniel St
Aborn St

Eustis Ave

Gibbs Ave

Old Beach Rd

Bliss Mine Rd

Acacia Dr S
Guthrie St
Barbara St
Kay St
Kay Blvd
Bliss Mine Rd
Friends Dr

Eastons North Pond

Eastons South Pond

Memorial Blvd

Easton Bay

Dennison St
Young St
Howard St
Pope St
S Baptist St
Dearborn St

Dean Ave
Lee Ave

Walnut Wharf

Jones Ave

Bowery St
E Bowery St
Berkeley Ave
Perry St

Bellevue Ct

Weaver Ave
Easton Rd
Faxon Green Rd
Gammell Rd

Morton Rd
Seaview Ave

Cliff Ave

Sylvan Ter
Parker Ave

McAllister St
Dixon St

Ward Ave

Wellington Ave

Chastellux Ave

Halidon Ave

Pea Craig

Rosenbeath Ave

Clinton St
Houston Ave

Marchant St

Connection St
Atlantic St
Eastnor Rd

Harrison Ave

Harrison Ln

Carroll Ave

Thames St

Morton Ave

Spring St

Howe Ave

Hazard Ave

Morton Park

Bellevue Ave

Narragansett Ave

Webster St

Narragansett Ave

Salve Regina University

Ochre Point Ave

© 2006 MapQuest, Inc.

©2006 NAVTEQ

0   300m
900ft

* St. Michael's Country Day School

The MapQuest logo is a registered trademark of MapQuest, Inc.
Map content (c) 2006 by MapQuest, Inc. and NavTeq.
The MapQuest trademarks and all content are used with permission.

120

Recipe Index

Appetizers

Black Bean Fritters with a Tropical Vinaigrette, 86
Brie and Cherry Pastry Cups, 20
Caponata, 87
Crab Stuffed Bacon Wrapped Shrimp, 21
Fresh Tomato Salsa, 70
Gi-Gi's Crab Cakes, 70
Ginger Scented Pecans, 44
Gravlax, 83
Gruyere and Parmesan Croustillants with
       Lavendar Salt, 71
Guacamole, Perfected, 85
Hot Lobster Dip, 83
Huitres Vivarois, 93
Lobster Martini, 33
Marinated Shrimp Wrapped in Snow Peas, 44
Olive-Goat Cheese Bruschetta, 85
Portugese Littlenecks, 56
Prosciutto and Gruyere Pinwheels, 92
Smoked Salmon Wraps, 87
Spicy Black Bean Salsa, 71
Summer Shrimp, 82
Tuna Tartare, 93

Beverages

Homemade Pink Lemonade, 66
Lemonade by the Sea, 52
Spiced Pear Bloody Mary Mix, 32

Breads and Pastry

Auntie Pam's Banana Bread, 10
Best-Ever Blueberry Muffins, 11
Fruit and Nut Breakfast Bars, 11
Microbrew Beer Bread, 49
Streusel Coffee Cake, 10

Breakfast Dishes

Cajun Breakfast Casserole, 15
Creamy Strawberry French Toast, 13
Gaufrettes, 13,
Spinach and Cheese Mini Quiche, 16
Torta Rustica, 14

Soups

Chilled Fruit Soup with Fresh Mint, 33
Chilled Gazpacho, 56
Clam Chowder, 112
Fresh Mushroom Soup, 20
New England Corn Chowder with Lobster, 82
Norey's Fabulous Corn Chowder, 32
Zucchini Watercress Soup, 92

Salads

Baby Spinach Salad with Warm Goat Cheese Medallions, 22
Cold Beef Salad Vinaigrette, 73
Corn Salad, 63
Jazzy Chicken Salad, 45
Lemon Artichoke Salad, 45
Mid-Summer Night's Salad, 97
Provencal Potato Salad, 47
Roasted Fig and Arugula Salad, 94
Roasted Green Bean, Red Onion and Beet Salad, 72
Salad of Potatoes, Avocado and Watercress, 22
Spinach Salad with Warm Bacon, Mushrooms and Citrus
       Compote, 57
Summer Fruit Salad with Mint Sugar, 16
Sweet Summer Salad, 34
Warm Heirloom Tomato and Crispy Mozzarella Salad, 94
Watermelon Tomato Salad, 34
Wild Rice Salad, 39

Fish and Seafood

Grilled Marinated Shrimp with Mango Lime Relish, 35
Grilled Shrimp with Scallops over Wilted Baby Spinach
        with a Sweet Corn and Basil Coulis, 61
Grilled Striped Bass with Corn, Tomatoes and
        Green Beans, 62
Lobster Fatulli, 95
Mid-Summer Night's Salad, 97
Pan Seared Scallops with Orange Mascarpone Sauce, 98
Sea Salt Crusted Tuna with Shallot Cream Sauce, 101
Sea Scallops with Pear, Endive, and Maytag Bleu Cheese, 37
Seared Local Striped Bass with Apricot Quinoa and
        Mushroom Fennel Vinaigrette, 99
Spinach Stuffed Sole with Lemon Zest Sauce, 25
Tenderloin Stuffed with Lobster, 96
Traditional Newport Clambake for 20, 110

Meats and Poultry

Barbecue Chicken, 59
Grilled Ginger and Peppercorn Flank Steak, 57
Kobe Beef Burger, 58
Lemon Chicken, 75
Sautéed Chicken Breasts with Balsamic Vinegar Sauce, 38
Spicy Supercrunchy Fried Chicken, 46
Tenderloin Stuffed with Lobster, 96
The Best Ribs Ever, 46

Sandwiches

Nutty Cucumber Sandwich, 75

Pasta and Rice

Basil Summer Pasta, 64
Creamy Two-Cheese Polenta, 38
Nutted Wild Rice, 49
Spinach Lasagna Special, 73
Wild Mushroom Risotto, 103
Wild Rice Salad, 39

Vegetable Side Dishes

Café Green Beans, 39
Carrots with Minted Mustard Vinaigrette, 76
Dutch Style Belgian Endive, 25
Grilled Artichokes with Olive Oil, Lemon, and Mint, 102
Grilled Asparagus with Balsamic Vinegar, 101
Grilled Baby Eggplant with Red Pepper Sauce, 77
Grilled Summer Squash, 63
Pesto Green Beans with Three Types of Tomatoes, 76
Spinach Soufflé, 27
Sweet Minty Carrots, 26
Tricolor Potatoes with Pesto Parmesan, 102
Vegetarian Quinoa Casserole, 26
Zucchini Tomatoes Sauté, 64

Desserts

Banana Split Cake, 78
Chocolate Decadence, 104
Coconut Cream Pie, 27
Coconut Macaroons, 88
Creamy Blueberry Pie, 40
Creole Bread Pudding, 50
Fresh Blueberry Pie, 65
Gingersnaps, 51
Great Grandma's Boston Creams, 77
Heaven Cream, 65
Incredible Edibles, 66
Lemon Bars, 78
Lemon Granita, 103
Lemon Meringue Pie, 28
Macadamia Lime Pie, 51
Simple Simon's Frozen Pieman's Yogurt Pie, 40
Strawberries with Strawberry Sauce over Ice Cream, 66
Summer Fruit Salad with Mint Sugar, 16
Summer Peach Crisp, 28
Toblerone Chocolate Mousse, 88
Turtle Bars, 52
Vanilla Roasted Strawberries, 104
Watermelon with Mango and Lime, 50

Give "Flavors of a Newport Summer" to a Friend

Order by Mail:

Please send me __ copies of Flavors of a Newport Summer.
$16.95 (plus $4 shipping and handling fee) for each copy .
Total Payment Enclosed: $ _____

Ship To:
Name: _____
Mailing Address: _____
City, State, Zip: _____
Phone number: _____
Email address: _____

Form of Payment: Check or Credit Card

Mail check payable to:
SMCDS Parents Association

Credit Card: Visa or Mastercard
Account Number: _____
Expiration Date: _____
Name on card: _____
Billing Address: _____
City, State, Zip: _____

Mail completed order form to:

St. Michael's Country Day School
180 Rhode Island Avenue
Newport, RI 02840
Telephone: (401) 849-5970

Order Online:
We accept PayPal

Visit www.stmichaelscountryday.org/community

Click on the Parents Association PayPal link
(please provide mailing address on PayPal payment screen)

PayPal®